BOOK 2 - Timpani & Auxiliary Percussion

STANDARD OF EXCELLENCE

COMPREHENSIVE BAND METHOD

By Bruce Pearson

Dear Student:

Congratulations! You have successfully attained the first level in achieving a standard of excellence in music-making. By now, you have discovered that careful study and regular practice have brought you the joy and satisfaction of making beautiful music.

You are now ready to move to the next level in your music-making. I want to welcome you to STANDARD OF EXCELLENCE Book 2. I also want to wish you continued success and enjoyment.

Best wishes,

Bruce Pearson

Practicing - the key to EXCELLENCE!

▶ Make practicing part of your daily schedule. If you plan practicing as you do any other activity, you will find plenty of time for it.
▶ Try to practice in the same place every day. Choose a place where you can concentrate on making music. Start with a regular and familiar warm-up routine. Like an athlete, you need to warm-up your mind and muscles before you begin performing.
▶ Set goals for every practice session. Keep track of your practice time and progress on the front cover Practice Journal.
▶ Practice the hard spots in your lesson assignment and band music over and over, until you can play them perfectly.
▶ At the end of each practice session, play something fun.

SPECIAL NOTE: Pages 42-43, 46, and 48 are not included in this book. When the band is playing from pages 42-43, use the STANDARD OF EXCELLENCE Drums and Mallet Percussion Book.

*The author wishes to thank percussionist **Sam Lutfiyya** for his contributions to this book.*

ISBN 0-8497-5971-4

© 1994 Neil A. Kjos Music Company, 4380 Jutland Drive, San Diego, California.
International copyright secured. All rights reserved. Printed in the U.S.A.
WARNING! Governments around the world provide copyright laws to encourage composition and publication of new music. Anyone copying this music without permission is breaking the copyright law and is subject to penalties. Please do not violate copyright laws. Do not copy or reproduce the contents of this book in any way. **Thank you!**

kjos NEIL A. KJOS MUSIC COMPANY, PUBLISHER   W22TM

REVIEW

B♭ MAJOR KEY SIGNATURE

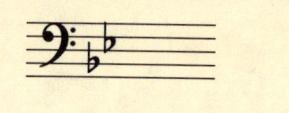

1 WARM-UP - Tacet

2 B♭ MAJOR SCALE SKILL

▶ Lines with a medal are *Achievement Lines*. The chart on page 47 can be used to record your progress.

3 BOTANY BAY   Page 40 ▶

Australian Folk Song

▶ Be sure to strike the Tri. with a light, quick wrist motion on either the outside right hand corner near the top (△) or the inside right hand corner of the base (△).

▶ When you see a page number followed by an arrow, *Excellerate* to the page indicated for additional studies.

4 DRIVE TIME

▶ Hold the Tamb. head side up at an angle to the floor. Strike the head near the edge.

5 SHEPHERD'S HEY

English Folk Song

▶ To create the Tri. rolls, quickly move the beater back and forth at either connected corner of the Tri.

W22TM

REVIEW

E♭ MAJOR KEY SIGNATURE

6 E♭ MAJOR SCALE SKILL

7 MOLLY MALONE

Irish Folk Song

8 NO LOOKING BACK

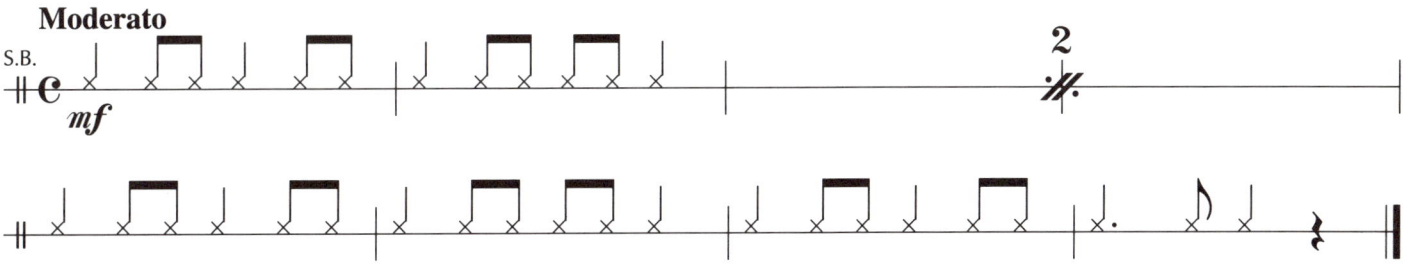

▶ Hold the handle of the S.B. in one hand with the bells pointing toward the floor. Make a fist with your other hand and firmly hit the upper end of the S.B.

9 TURKISH MARCH

Wolfgang Amadeus Mozart (1756 - 1791)

10 HYMN OF THANKSGIVING - Band Arrangement

Johann Crüger (1598 - 1662)
arr. Bruce Pearson (b. 1942)

REVIEW

F MAJOR KEY SIGNATURE

DAMPENING (MUFFLING) THE TIMPANI

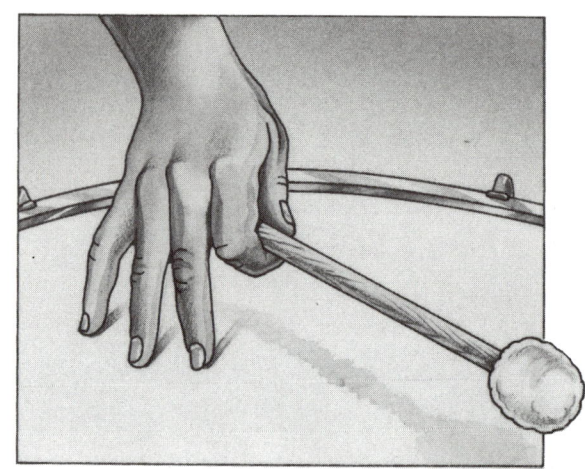

STEP 1
Strike the drum as you normally would, and allow the note to sustain for its full value.

STEP 2
If a rest follows the note, or if the note occurs at the end of the piece, dampen the drum by placing your third, fourth, and fifth fingers on the head. Your thumb and index finger should continue to hold the mallet throughout the dampening process. You may dampen with whichever hand is most convenient.

STEP 3
If both drums are struck just prior to a rest or the end of the piece, dampen the high drum with your right hand and the low drum with your left hand at the same time.

STEP 4
Try to dampen in the same spot that you struck the head, and apply enough pressure to stop the sound completely. Louder playing requires more pressure. When playing very loudly, it may be necessary to also use the heel of your hand to completely dampen the drum(s).

11 WARM-UP - Tacet

12 F MAJOR SCALE SKILL

13 KNUCKLEBUSTER - Tacet

14 GIVE ME THAT OLD TIME RELIGION

American Spiritual

▶ The S. Cym. and W. Blk. may be played by one percussionist. If so, place the W. Blk. on a soft, flat surface.

15 _____ Composer _____

your name

▶ Using the pitches F and C and any rhythms you know, compose an ending for this melody. Title and play your composition.

16 FOR TIMPANI ONLY   Page 40 ▶

▶ Dampen on rests using the hand indicated in parentheses.

SYNCOPATION

A rhythmic effect which places emphasis on a weak or unaccented part of the measure.

17 SYNCOPATION SENSATION

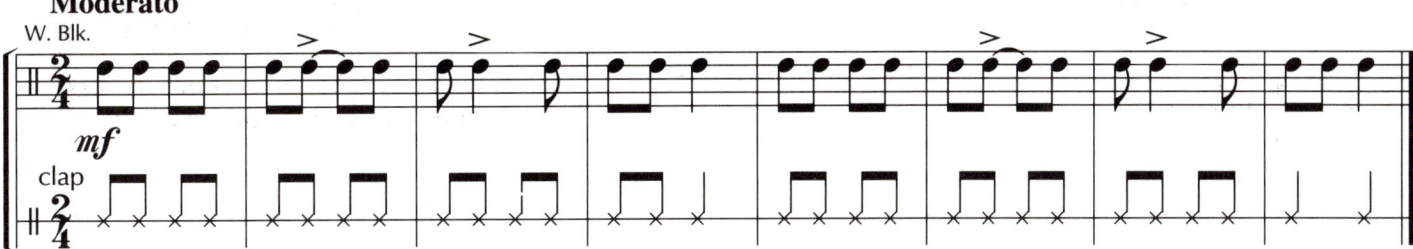

▶ Play the W. Blk. using two mallets.

18 THE RIDDLE SONG

American Folk Song

▶ Write in the counting and clap the rhythm before you play.

19 NOBODY KNOWS THE TROUBLE I'VE SEEN

American Spiritual

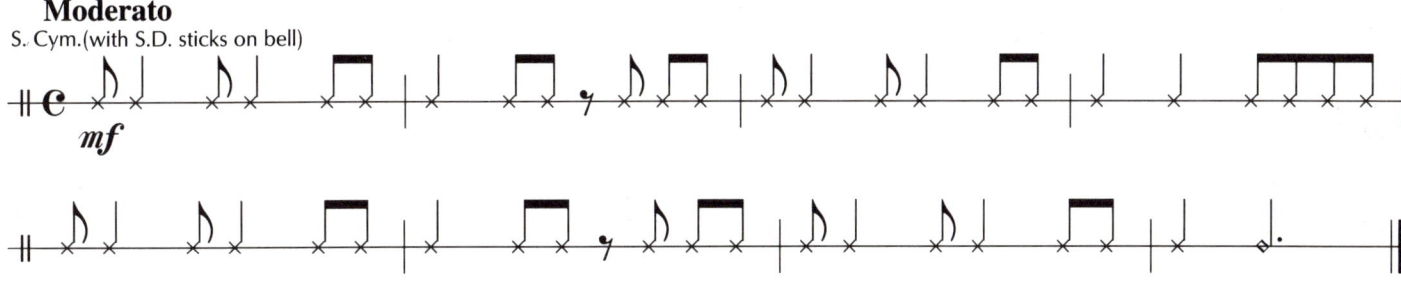

20 INTERVAL INQUIRY - Tacet   Page 40

▶ See the Standard of Excellence Drums & Mallet Percussion Book, "Mallets" page 5.

21 GO FOR EXCELLENCE!

American Folk Song

Allegro
"Liza Jane"
Timp. **F & B♭**

G MINOR KEY SIGNATURE	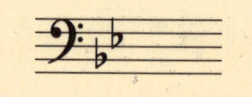	**G minor** has the same key signature as **B♭ major**.
TEMPO		*Accelerando (accel.)* - Gradually increase the tempo.

22 WARM-UP - Band Arrangement

▶ Play the high block with your right hand and the low block with your left hand. Strike the blocks on the top center of each block, using the same down-up wrist motion you use when playing W. Blk.

23 G NATURAL MINOR SCALE SKILL

▶ Dampen on rests using the hand(s) indicated in parentheses. When both hands are indicated, dampen both drums (low drum with the left hand and high drum with the right hand). Also, dampen at the end of the fermata.

24 G HARMONIC MINOR SCALE SKILL

▶ Dampen on rests using the hand(s) indicated in parentheses.

25 MINKA, MINKA

Ukrainian Folk Song

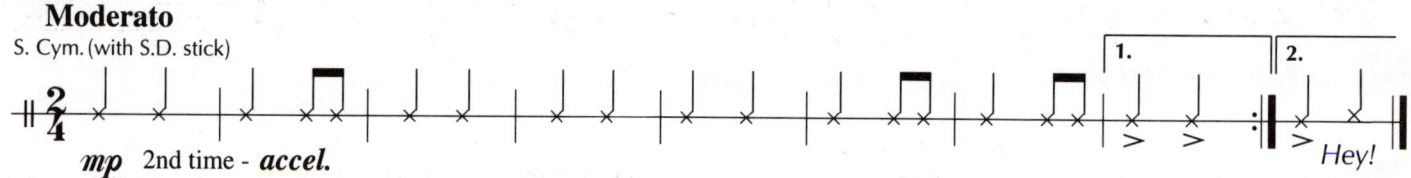

26 LAREDO - Duet

Mexican Folk Song

▶ Be sure to use proper techniques when playing Marc. or Claves.

6, cont.

SLUR 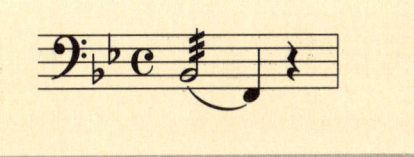 A slur is a curved line that connects two or more notes of <u>different</u> pitch.

Playing Rolled Timpani Notes Involving Slurs

STEP 1
Sustain the rolled note(s) for their maximum value.

STEP 2
When moving from note to note, move only one hand at a time. Move the hand closest to the destination drum <u>while</u> the other hand finishes the roll on the original drum. Move as smoothly as possible, allowing no break between slurred notes.

27. TURNING YOU LOOSE

▶ Dampen on rests using the hand indicated in parentheses.

28. FOR TIMPANI ONLY — Page 40

▶ Dampen on rests using the hand(s) indicated in parentheses.

W22TM

LET VIBRATE (L.V.)		Let the instrument ring; do not dampen.
DAL SEGNO AL FINE (D.S. AL FINE)		Go back to the sign (𝄋) and play until the *Fine*.

JOYEUX NOËL
Band Arrangement

French Carol
arr. Chuck Elledge (b. 1961)

Tambourine
Triangle

7B

LET VIBRATE (L.V.)		Let the instrument ring; do not dampen.
DAL SEGNO AL FINE (D.S. AL FINE)		Go back to the sign (𝄋) and play until the *Fine*.

JOYEUX NOËL
Band Arrangement

Suspended Cymbal
Crash Cymbals

French Carol
arr. Chuck Elledge (b. 1961)

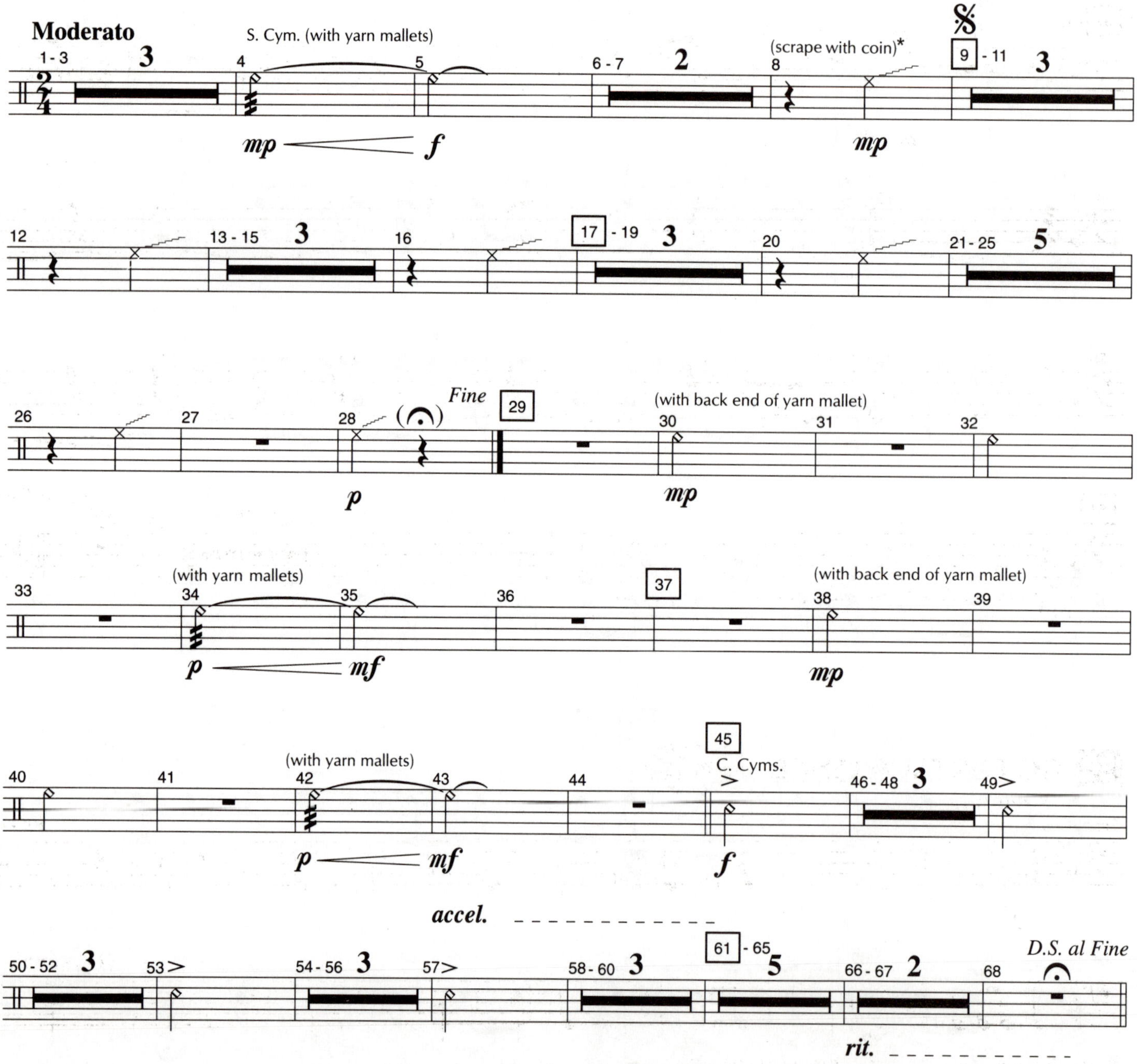

*Scrape the S. Cym. with a coin, starting at the bell and moving toward the edge.

W22TM

DAL SEGNO AL FINE (D.S. AL FINE)

Go back to the sign (𝄋) and play until the ***Fine.***

JOYEUX NOËL

Band Arrangement

Timpani

French Carol
arr. Chuck Elledge (b. 1961)

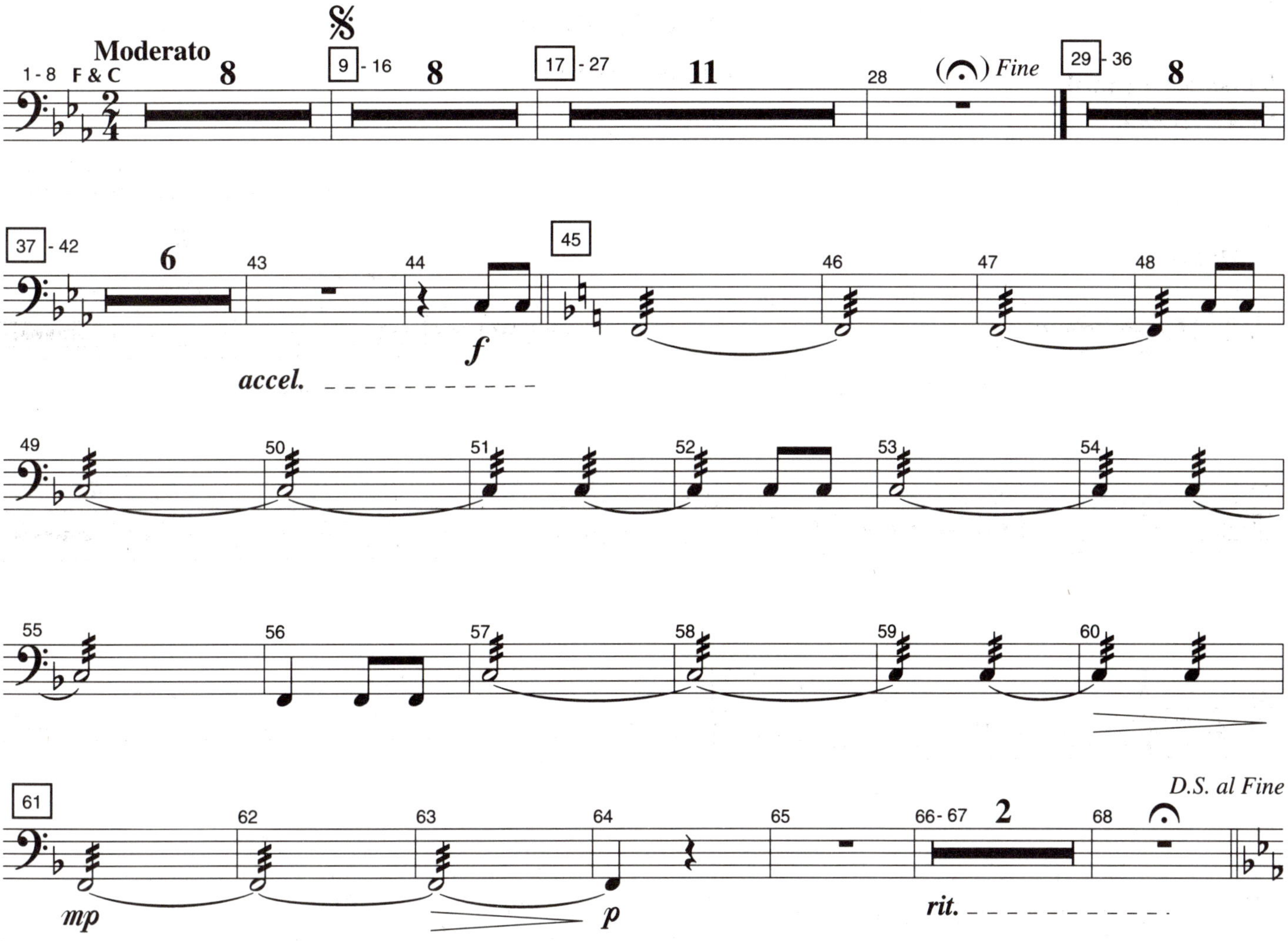

29 GO FOR EXCELLENCE!

Moderato

Timp. **G & D**

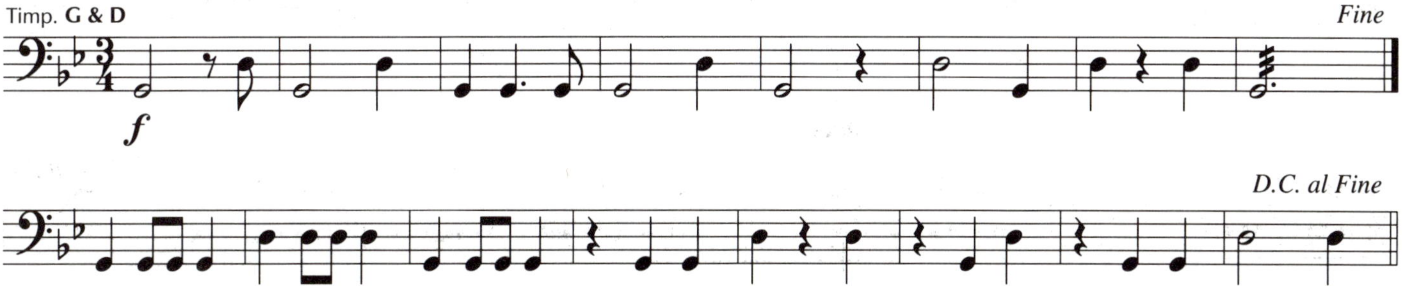

▶ End the roll when the rest of the band cuts off.

30 EIGHTH REST ON THE BEAT
Moderato
W. Blk.

mf

▶ Write in the counting and clap the rhythm before you play.

31 EIGHTH REST OFF THE BEAT
Moderato
Tamb.

f

32 ACADEMIC FESTIVAL MARCH - Trio

Johannes Brahms (1833 - 1897)

Moderato

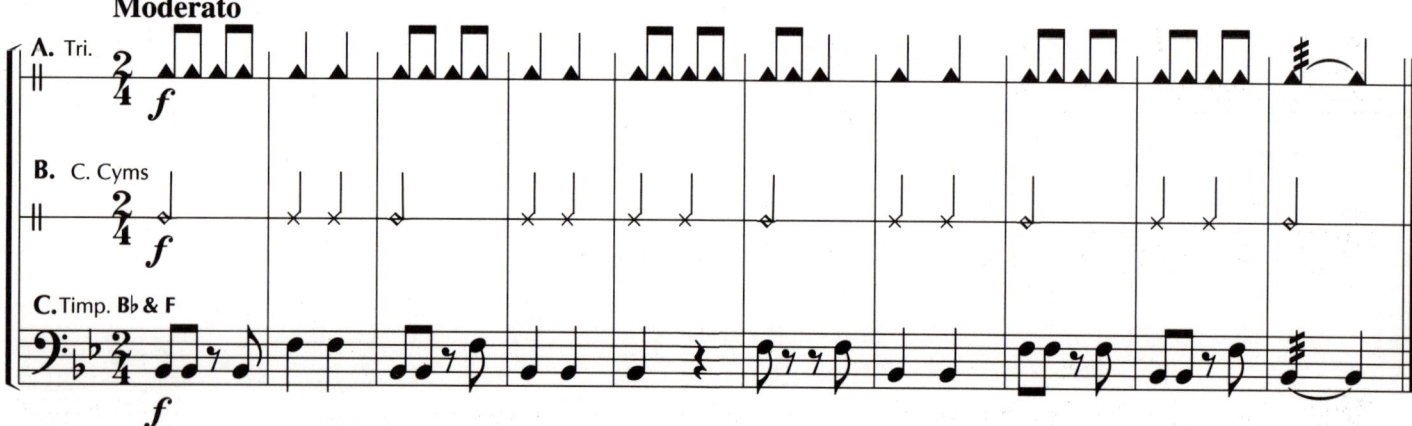

33 BREEZIN'
Allegro
S. Cym. (with yarn mallets)

p

▶ Dampen the S. Cym. on the rests.

34 YANKEE DOODLE - Duet

American Folk Song

Moderato

35 FOR TIMPANI ONLY

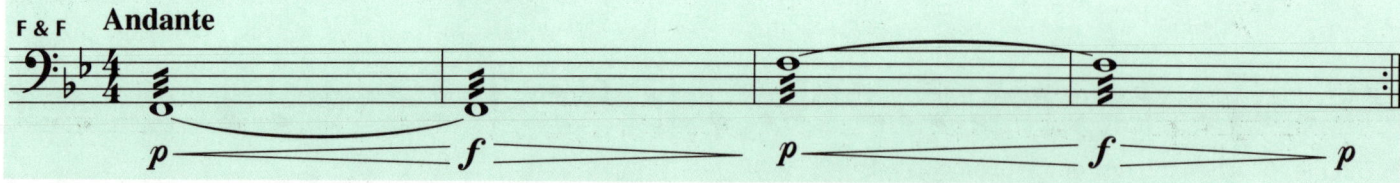

▶ Let the natural vibrations of the head create the sustained roll sound. In general, the lower the drum is tuned, the slower the strokes need to be. In this case, use slower strokes when playing low F than when playing high F.

W22TM

A♭ MAJOR KEY SIGNATURE

This key signature means play all B's as B flats, all E's as E flats, all A's as A flats, and all D's as D flats.

PLAYING A TAMBOURINE SHAKE ROLL

STEP 1
Hold the tambourine using your normal grip. With the tambourine in a vertical position, rotate your wrist to create the roll. The wrist motion should be similar to that used when turning a door knob.

STEP 2
For a cleaner articulation, begin the roll with a single stroke on the head with your free hand.

STEP 3
If the roll is tied to a single note, strike that note with your free hand as you stop the roll. Otherwise, simply stop the sound by rotating the tambourine to a position so that the head is parallel to the floor.

STEP 4
When you practice rolls, sometimes hold the tambourine in your right hand, and other times hold it in your left hand.

36 A♭ MAJOR SCALE SKILL

37 GREASED LIGHTNING

▶ Play the rolled notes using shake rolls. Strike the non-rolled notes with your free hand as you normally would.

38 PARTNER SONGS - Tacet

39 GO FOR EXCELLENCE!

Stephen Foster (1826 - 1864)

"Oh! Susanna"

▶ Be sure to dampen on the rests. Experiment with various stickings and dampenings and write in the sticking that works best for you.

W22TM

| TEMPO | **Allegretto** - light and lively; slightly slower than **Allegro**. |

40 WARM-UP - Tacet

41 CHROMATIC CAPERS

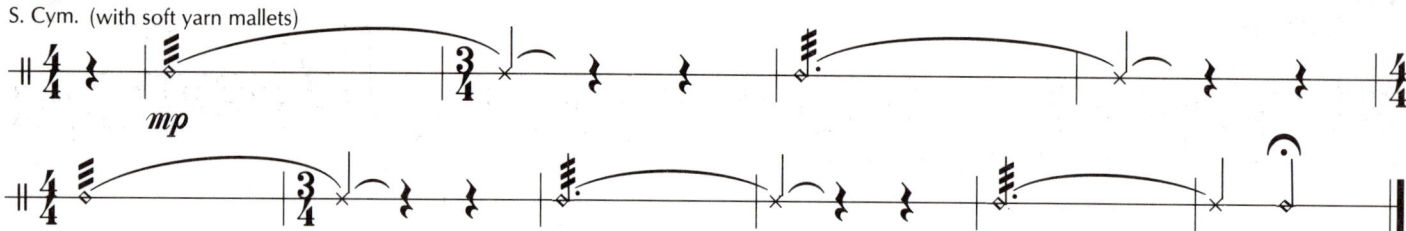

42 SHENANDOAH

American Folk Song

43 THEME FROM SYMPHONY NO. 94   Page 40

Franz Joseph Haydn (1732 - 1809)

▶ Dampen on rests using the hand(s) indicated in parentheses.

44 PARADE OF THE TIN SOLDIERS

Léon Jessel (1871 - 1942)

▶ This exercise may be played by one percussionist.

45 FOR TIMPANI ONLY

▶ Choose stickings which allow you to easily move from drum to drum and dampen on rests comfortably.

C MINOR KEY SIGNATURE

C minor has the same key signature as **E♭ major.**

ARTICULATION

Legato **-** Play as smoothly as possible.

46 C NATURAL MINOR SCALE / 47 C HARMONIC MINOR SCALE

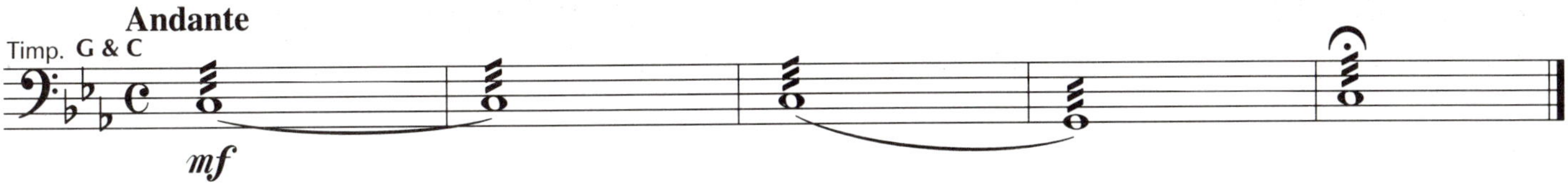

48 MARCHE SLAV

Peter Ilyich Tchaikovsky (1840 - 1893)

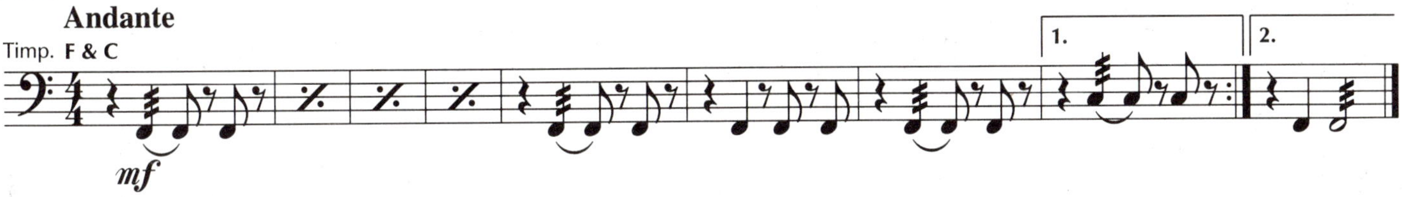

49 GREENSLEEVES

English Song

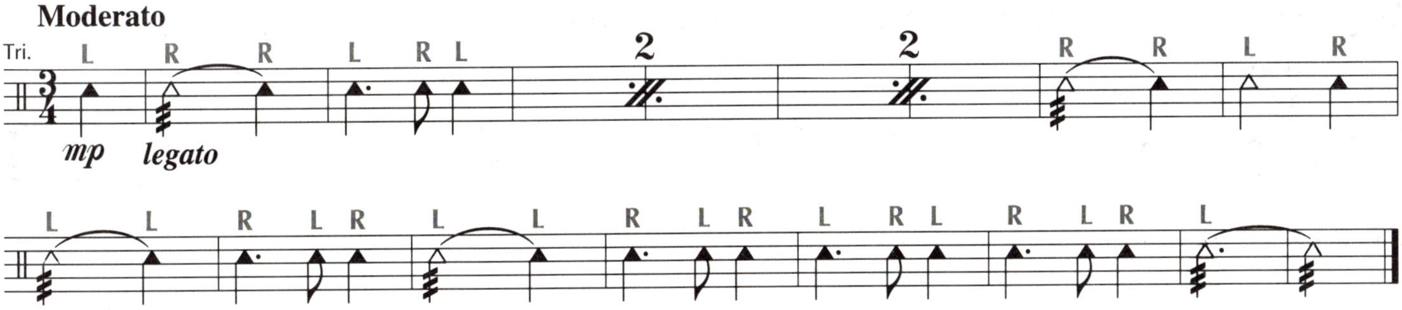

▶ Play this exercise using two beaters. Suspend the Tri. from a music stand using two clamps. Hold a beater in each hand and strike the Tri. on the top.

50 JUBILATE

Wolfgang Amadeus Mozart (1756 - 1791)

51 GO FOR EXCELLENCE!

▶ Play this exercise using two beaters.

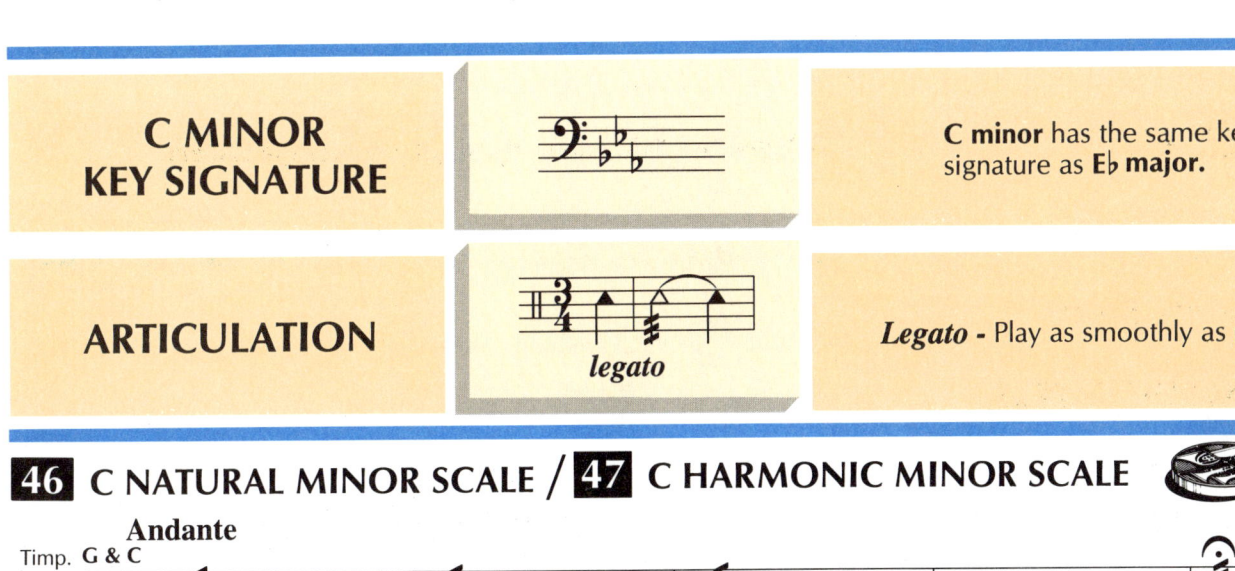

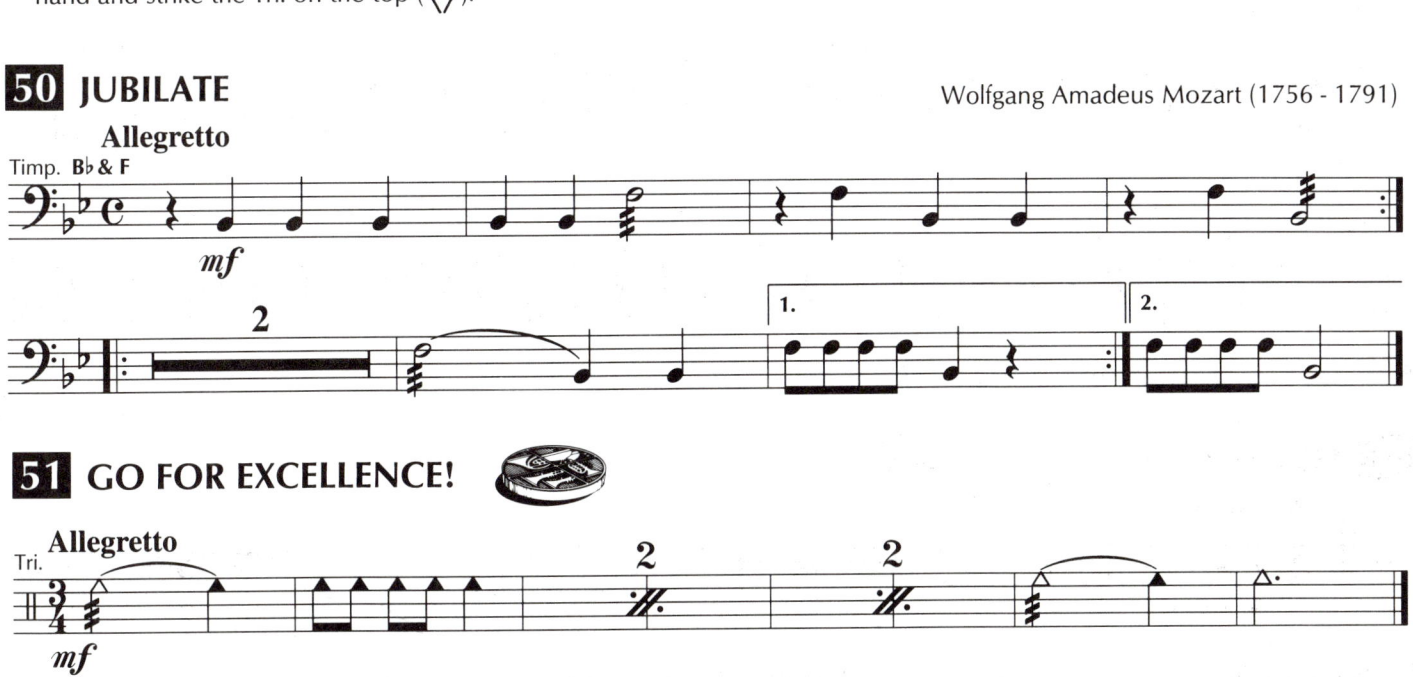

12

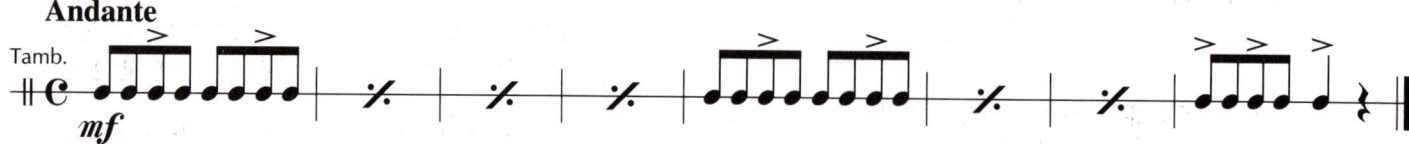

▶ Play the eighth notes by shaking the Tamb. with a back and forth fanning motion. Strike the Tamb. against your free hand on the accented notes.

▶ End the rolls when the rest of the band cuts off.

56 THE BRITISH GRENADIERS - Tacet

▶ Dampen on rests using the hand(s) indicated in parentheses.

W22TM

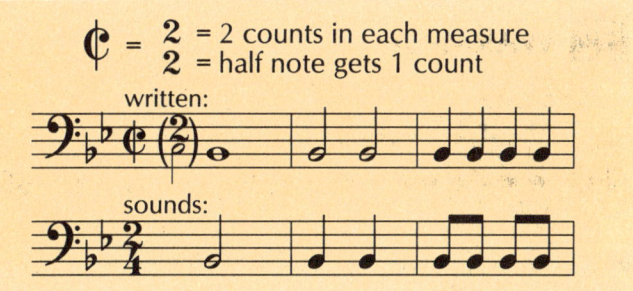

TIME SIGNATURE

This time signature is called **cut time** or *alla breve*.

58 CUT AND PASTE

▶ Write in the counting and clap the rhythm before you play.

59 OATS, PEAS, BEANS
American Folk Song

60 THE VICTORS
Fight Song
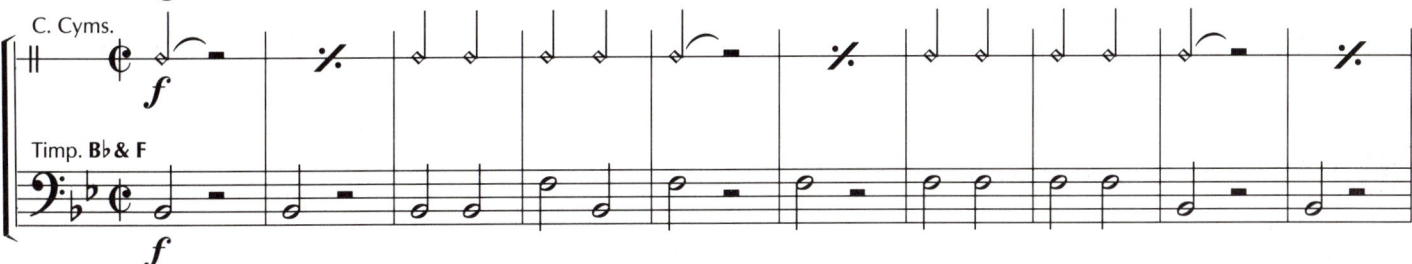

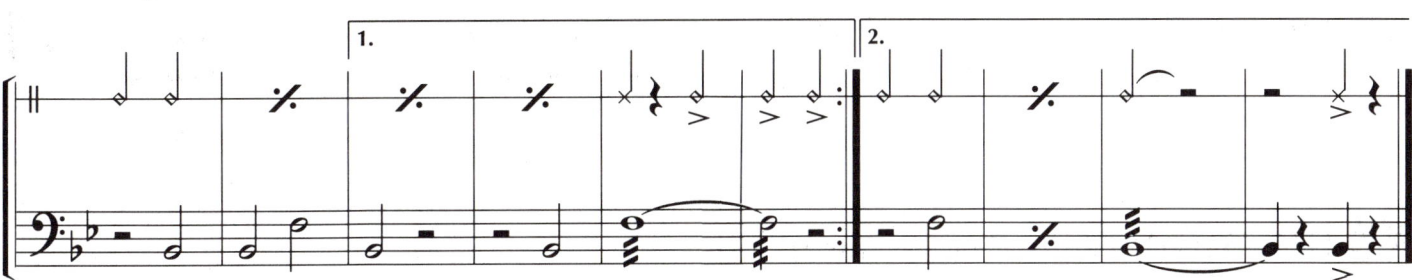

61 OVER EASY - Tacet

62 GO FOR EXCELLENCE!

John Philip Sousa (1854 - 1932)

"High School Cadets March"

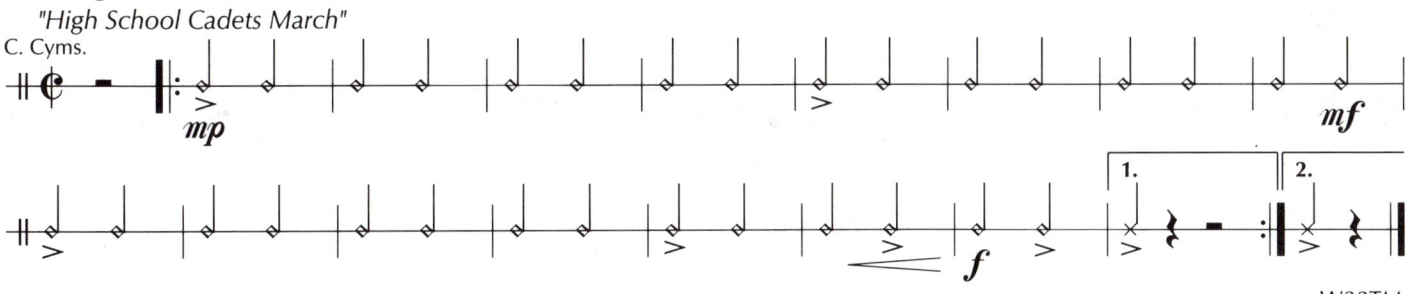

63 WARM-UP - Band Arrangement

64 DANISH ROLL
Danish Folk Song

▶ Play F with your left hand and C with your right hand in measures 1-2, 4-6, and 8.

65 RUSSIAN SAILORS' DANCE
Reinhold Glière (1875 - 1956)

▶ On the Tamb. rolls tied to a single note, strike the single note with your free hand as you stop the roll.

66 CHORD CAPERS - Tacet
▶ See the Standard of Excellence Drums & Mallet Percussion Book, "Mallets" page 14.

67 FOR TIMPANI ONLY

▶ Dampen both drums on the rests.

W22TM

THE BONGOS

PLAYING THE BONGOS

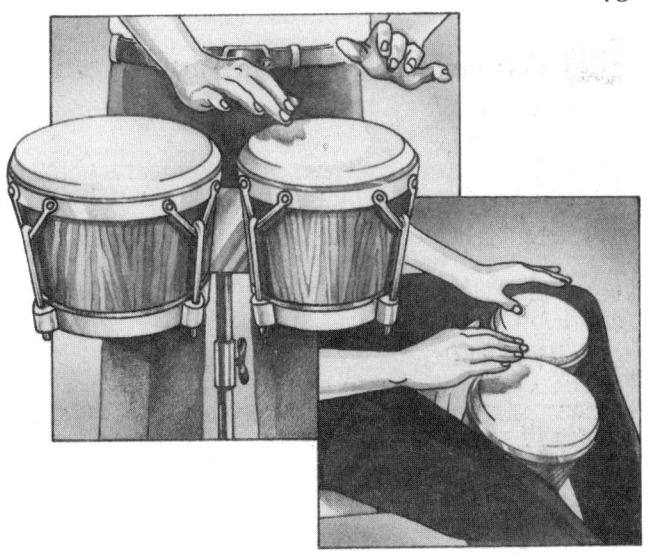

STEP 1
Sit on a chair or stool and hold the bongos between your knees. You may also mount the bongos on a stand, and play them from a standing position. The music you are playing will determine whether the small (higher pitched) drum should be to your left or to your right.

STEP 2
Strike the bongos with your fingers or thumbs using energetic motions. Strike near the edge for a bright, ringing tone and toward the center for a richer, more muffled tone. Sound variation may also be achieved using different types of strokes.

STEP 3
In some cases, playing the bongos with light-weight sticks or mallets is required, especially when a great deal of volume is necessary. Hold the sticks or mallets using the same grip you use when playing mallet percussion instruments.

68 CHROMATIC SCALE SKILL

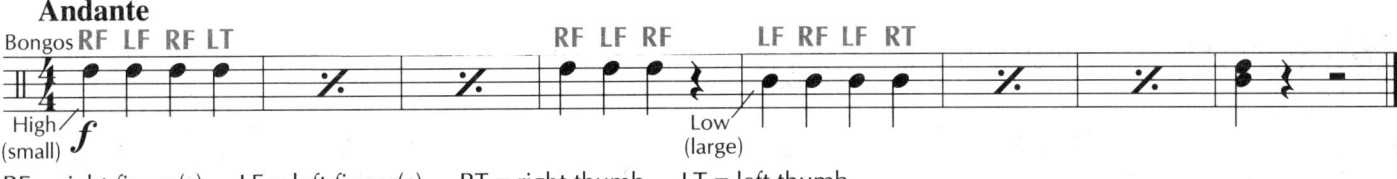

RF = right finger(s)   LF = left finger(s)   RT = right thumb   LT = left thumb

▶ Also try playing this exercise with your fingers only.

69 SAILING THE HIGH SEAS  Page 41

▶ Set up or hold the bongos with the small drum to your left and the large drum to your right. Also try playing this exercise with your fingers only.

70 CHROMATIC MARCH - Tacet

71 MANHATTAN BEACH MARCH

John Philip Sousa (1854 - 1932)

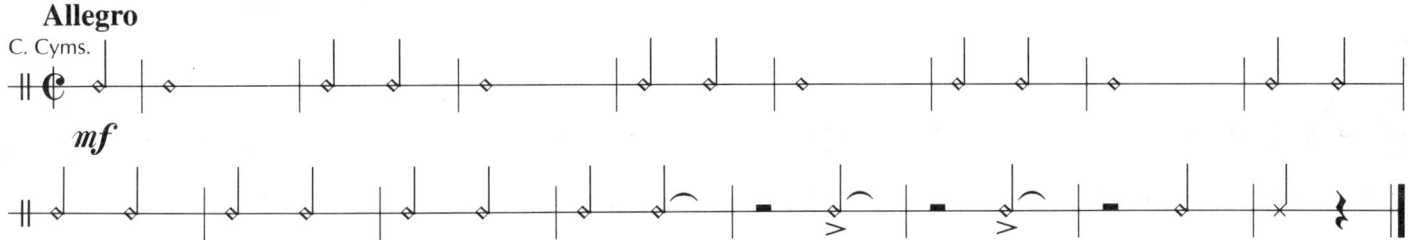

72 GO FOR EXCELLENCE!

▶ Experiment with various finger and thumb stroke combinations.

W22TM

17

TIME SIGNATURE

3/8

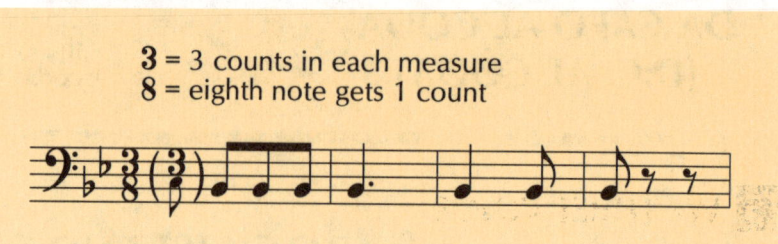

3 = 3 counts in each measure
8 = eighth note gets 1 count

73 **FINLANDIA - Band Arrangement**

Jean Sibelius (1865 - 1957)
arr. Bruce Pearson (b. 1942)

Moderato

Permission granted for sale outside of the U.S.A. by Breitkopf & Härtel.
© Breitkopf & Härtel, Wiesbaden, Germany

74 **TRIPLE PLAY**

▶ Write in the counting and clap the rhythm before you play.

W22TM

17, cont.

75 **WE THREE KINGS**
John H. Hopkins, Jr. (1820 - 1891)

▶ Name the key in "We Three Kings." _____

76 **GO FOR EXCELLENCE!**

C MAJOR KEY SIGNATURE

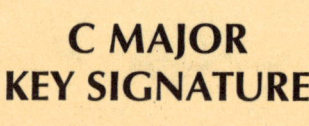

This key signature contains no sharps or flats.

TIME SIGNATURE

6 = 6 counts in each measure
8 = eighth note gets 1 count

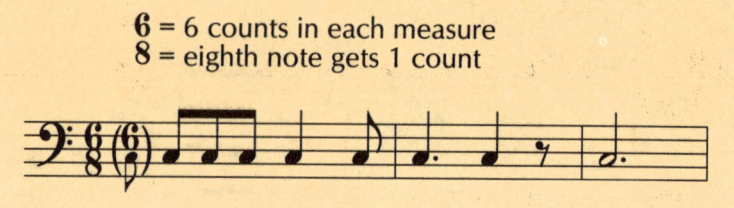

77 C MAJOR SCALE SKILL

▶ To create the Marc. roll in the last measure, shake the Marc. using fast alternating strokes.

78 OVER THE RIVER
Traditional

▶ Draw in a breath mark (') at the end of each phrase.

18, cont.

79 OODLES OF NOODLES

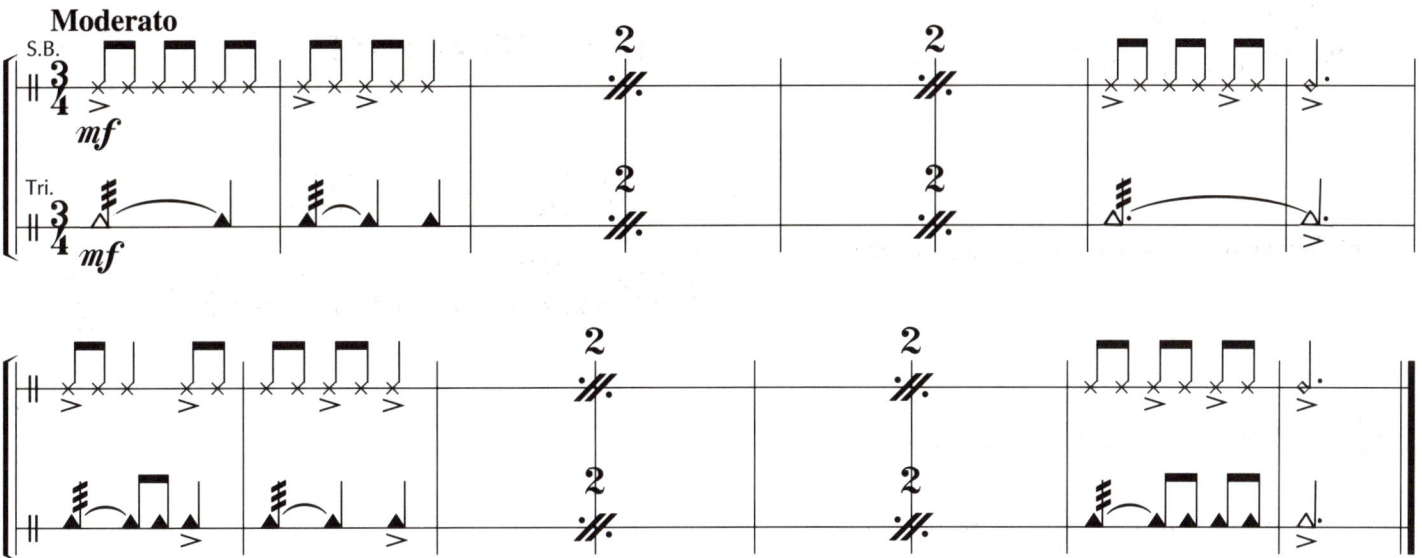

▶ To create the S.B. accents, strike your fist against the handle more forcefully than on the unaccented notes. Practice the Tri. part two ways: 1. With one beater; 2. With two beaters.

80 UPS AND DOWNS

▶ Write in the counting and draw in the bar lines before you play.

81 FOR TIMPANI ONLY

▶ Are you using even, relaxed strokes?

W22TM

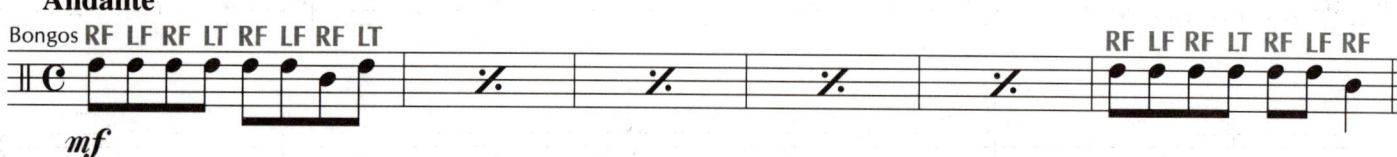

RF = right finger(s)   LF = left finger(s)   RT = right thumb   LT = left thumb

▶ Set up or hold the bongos with the small drum to your left and the large drum to your right.

▶ Use two mallets to play this exercise. Write in the counting and clap the rhythm before you play.

W22TM

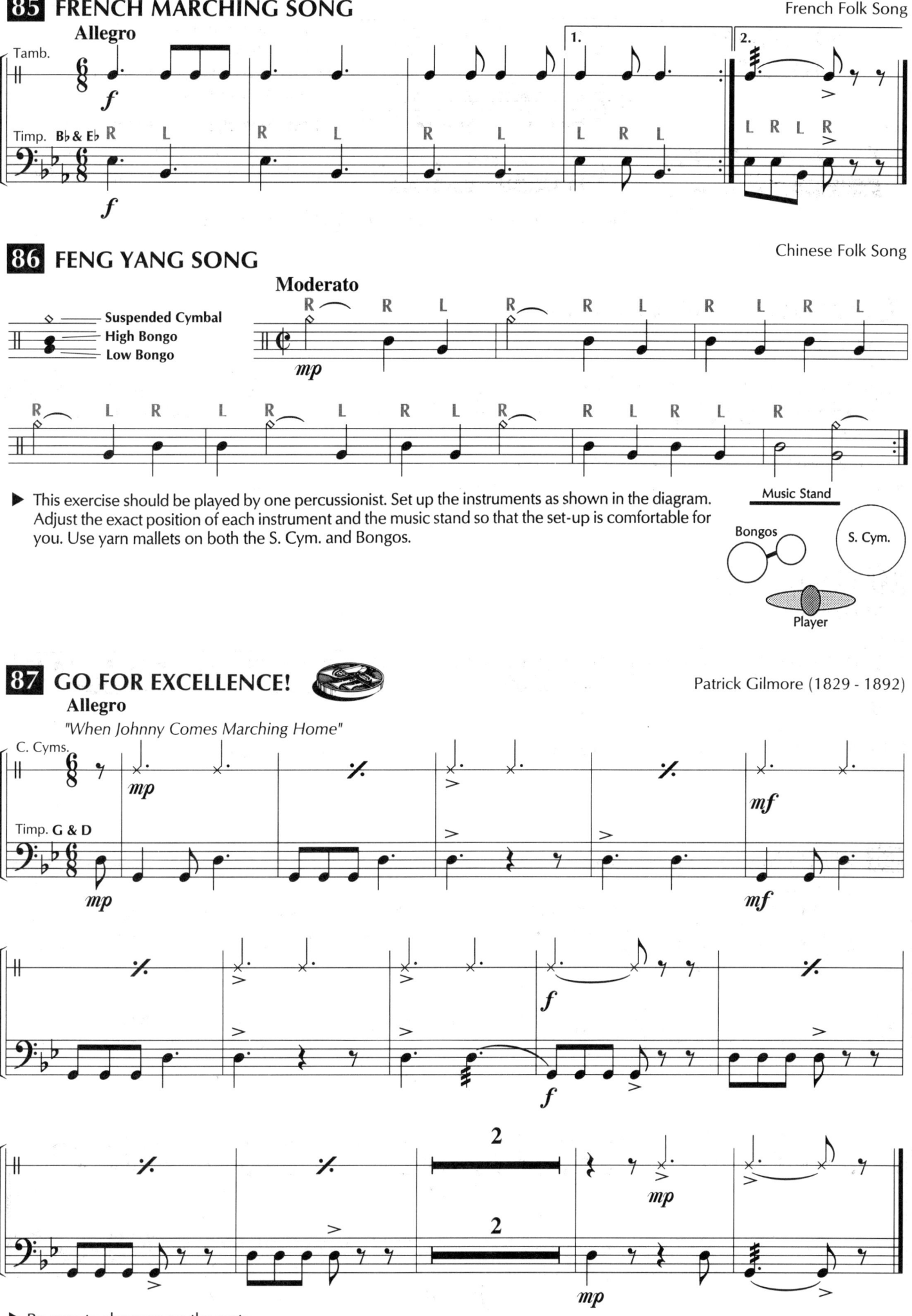

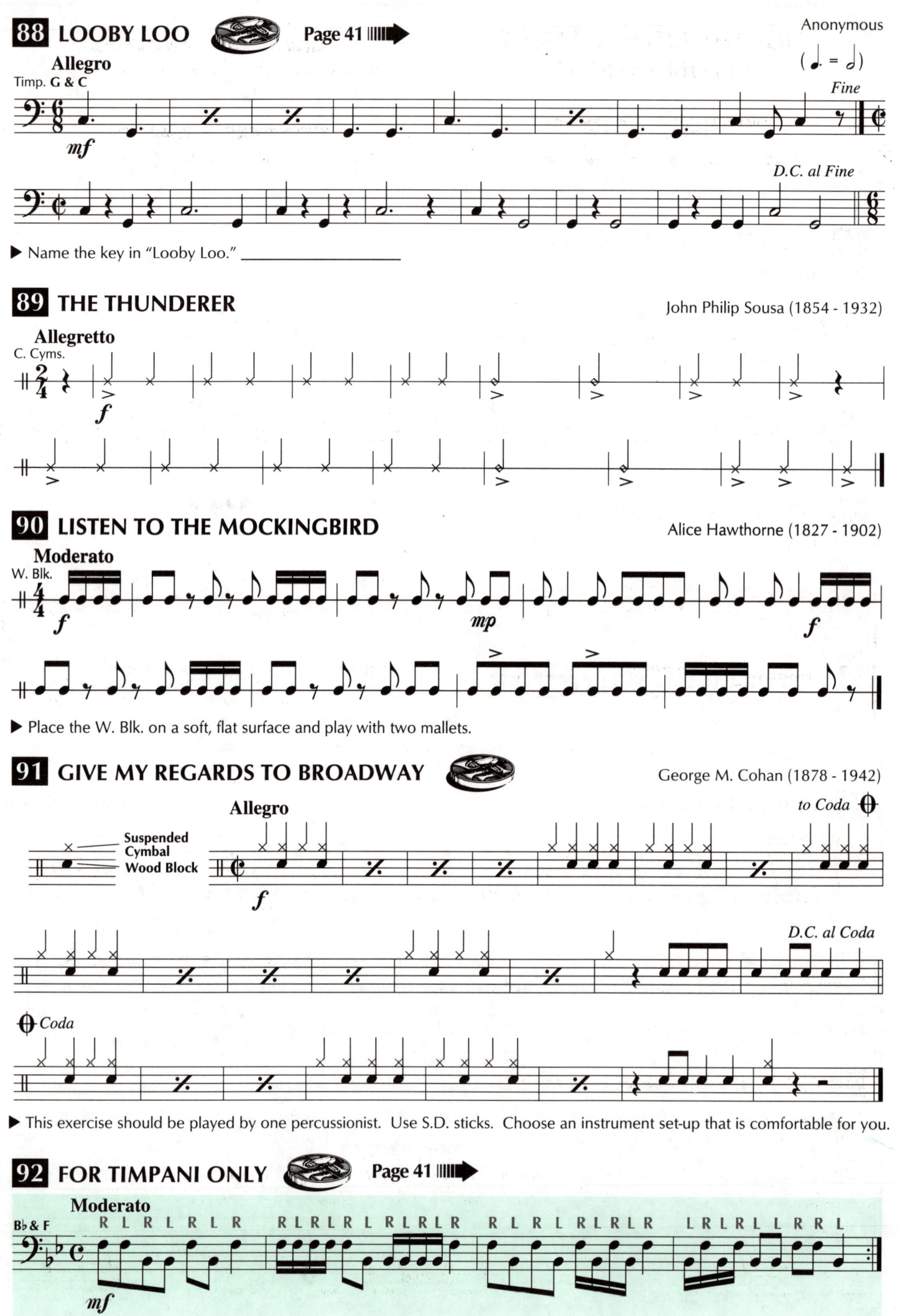

EIGHTH/SIXTEENTH NOTE COMBINATIONS

93 **CHESTER - Band Arrangement**

William Billings (1746 - 1800)
arr. Bruce Pearson (b. 1942)

94 **STEADY AS YOU GO - Duet**

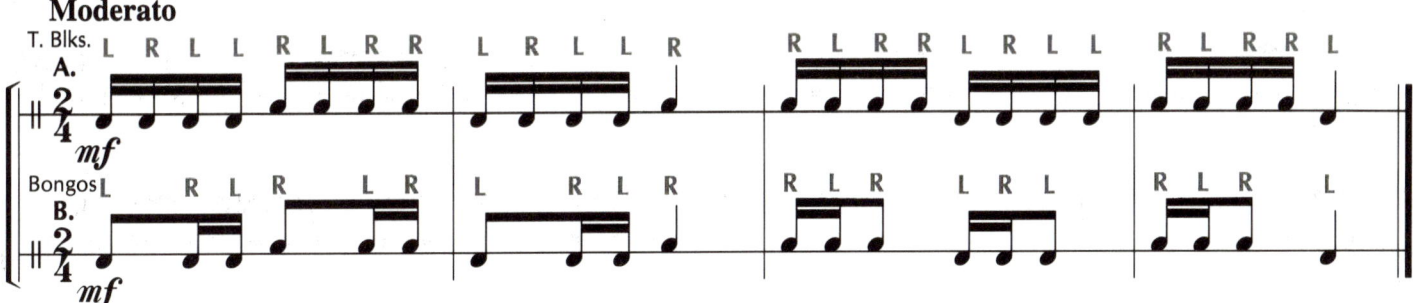

▶ Set up or hold the bongos with the small drum to your right and the large drum to your left.

95 **TIRRA LIRRA LOO**

Canadian Folk Song

▶ Play this exercise using two beaters. Write in the counting and clap the rhythm before you play.

96 **GO FOR EXCELLENCE!**

American Folk Song

"Big Rock Candy Mountain"

W22TM

TURKISH MARCH
from "The Ruins of Athens"
Percussion Ensemble

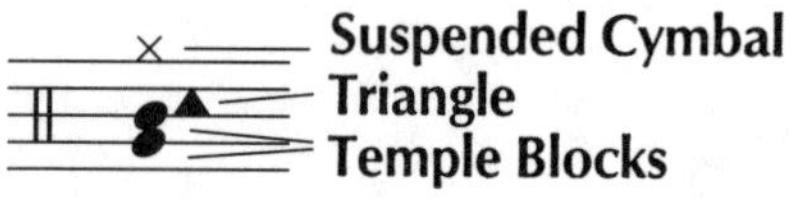

Ludwig van Beethoven (1770 - 1827)
arr. Bruce Pearson (b. 1942)

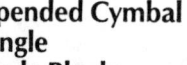
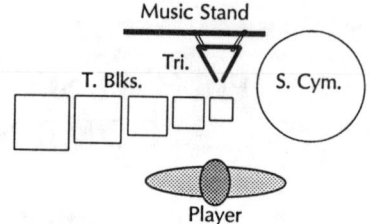

▶ This part should be played by one percussionist. Set up the instruments as shown in the diagram at the top of the page. Adjust the exact position of each instrument and the music stand so that the set-up is comfortable for you.
▶ Play the S. Cym. and T. Blks. with rubber mallets. Experiment with different pairs of blocks.
▶ Play the Tri. with two beaters.

W22TM

TURKISH MARCH
from "The Ruins of Athens"
Percussion Ensemble

Ludwig van Beethoven (1770 - 1827)
arr. Bruce Pearson (b. 1942)

Timpani

▶ Use medium hard timpani mallets to help achieve a clear sound. Separate the quarter note rolls in measures 15-16 and 43-44. Be sure to dampen on the rests throughout.

W22TM

SINGLE SIXTEENTH NOTE

A single sixteenth note is half as long as an eighth note.

♬ = ¼ count in 2/4, 3/4, and 4/4 time.

DOTTED EIGHTH NOTE

A dot after a note adds half the value of the note.

♪ + · = ♪ + ♪ = ♪.

DOTTED EIGHTH/SIXTEENTH NOTE COMBINATION

THE COWBELL (C.B.)

PLAYING THE COWBELL

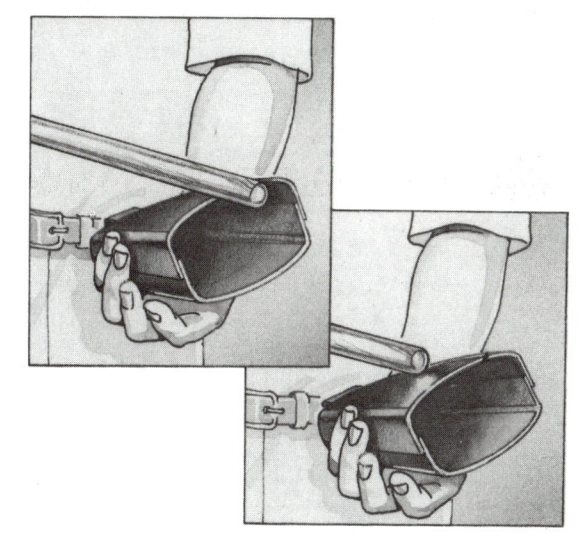

STEP 1
Rest the cowbell on the heel of one hand, with your thumb and little finger supporting the sides. Use your other three fingers for dampening, or to provide additional support if the cowbell is heavy or large.

STEP 2
In your other hand, hold a drum stick so that it is possible to play using the back end of the stick.

STEP 3
Strike the cowbell on the top edge of the mouth with the shaft of the stick, or on the top with the back end of the stick.

102 DOTS OF FUN

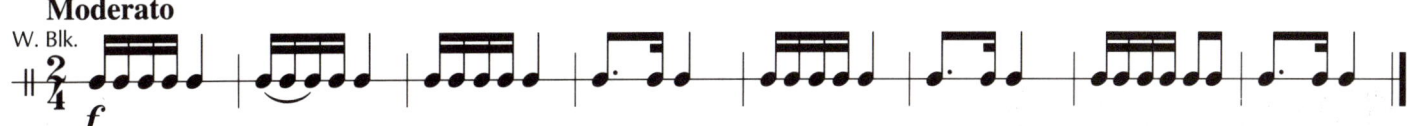

▶ Place the W. Blk. on a soft, flat surface. Play using two rubber mallets.

103 LITTLE BROWN JUG - Duet

Joseph Eastburn Winner (1837 - 1918)

▶ Write in the counting and clap the rhythm for the T. Blks. part before you play.

104 OUR BOYS WILL SHINE TONIGHT - Tacet / 105 - Tacet

106 GO FOR EXCELLENCE! Page 41

Georges Bizet (1838 - 1875)

"Farandole from L'Arlesienne Suite"

W22TM

107 CUCKOO SONG
Austrian Folk Song

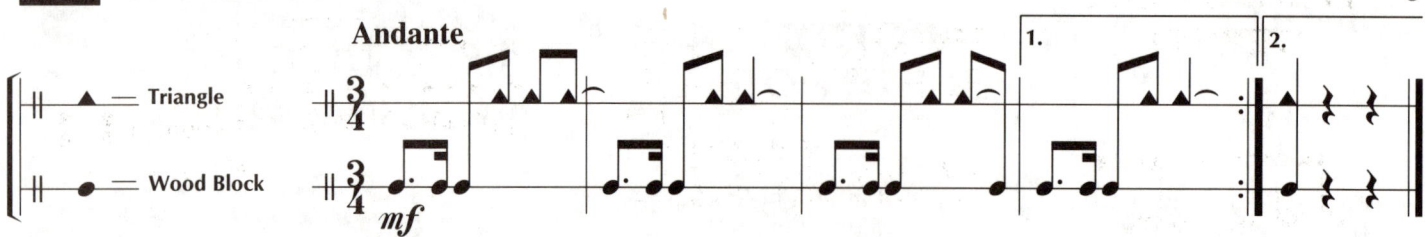

▶ This exercise may be played by one or two percussionists. If played by one, the W. Blk. should be placed on a soft, flat surface and played with a rubber mallet; the Tri. should be hung from a music stand and played with a Tri. beater.

108 MARCH MILITAIRE
Franz Schubert (1797 - 1828)

109 ST. ANTHONY CHORALE
Franz Joseph Haydn (1732 - 1809)

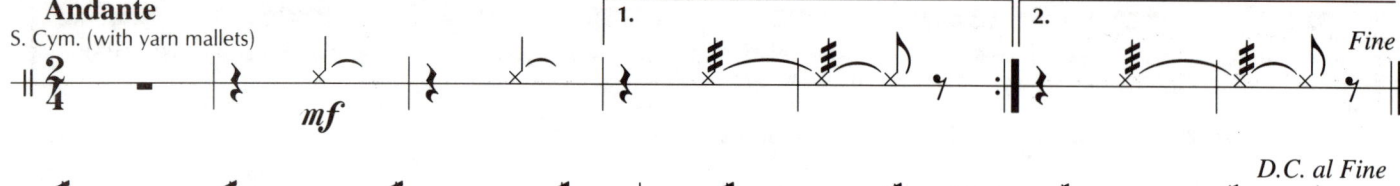
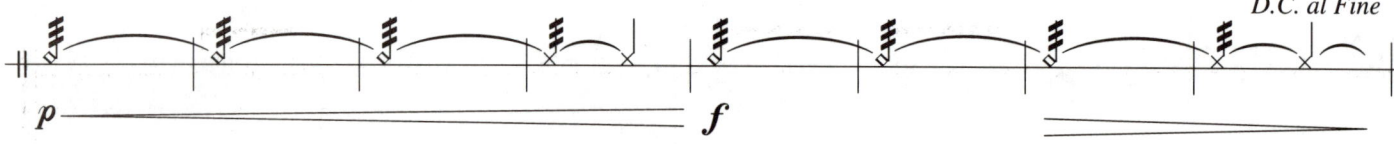

▶ On the rolls, alternate strokes only as fast as necessary to sustain the sound of the S. Cym. Striking the S. Cym. too often may deaden the sound.

110 - Tacet

111 FOR COWBELLS ONLY

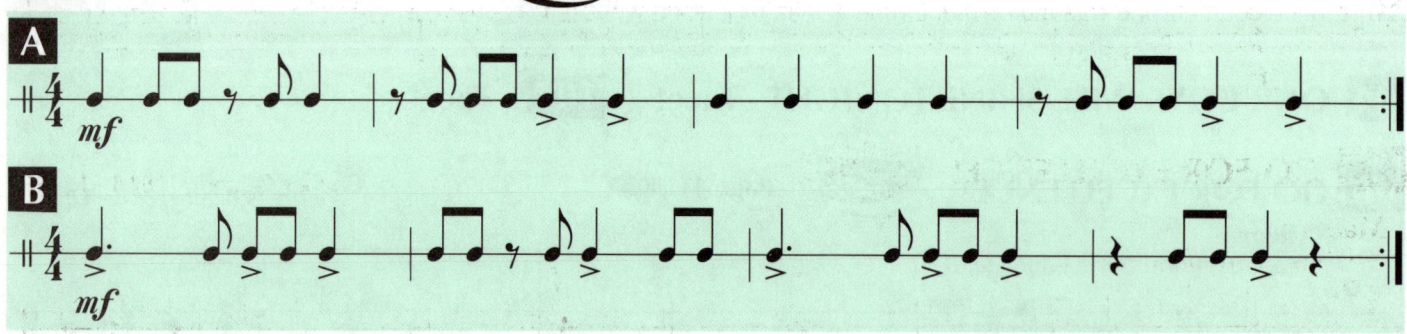

▶ Experiment with different sticks and mallets, and with different playing areas on the cowbell. Also try playing the cowbell on the top side with a clave.

W22TM

EIGHTH NOTE TRIPLET

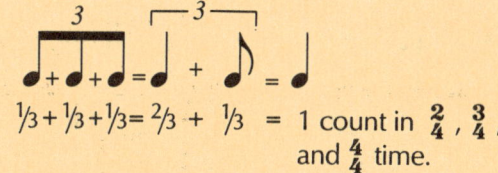

TEMPO

Maestoso - majestically

112 TRIPLE TREAT — Page 41

113 STARS OF THE HEAVENS - Duet — Mexican Folk Song
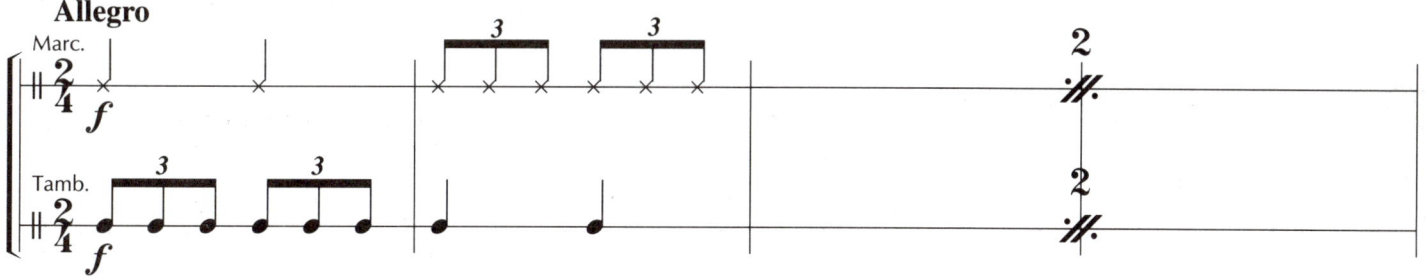
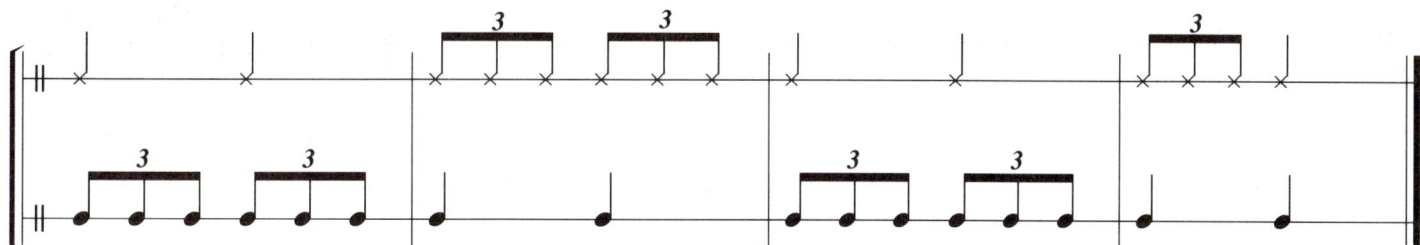

114 LIGHT CAVALRY OVERTURE — Franz von Suppé (1819 - 1895)

115 GO FOR EXCELLENCE!  — Charles Gounod (1818 - 1893)

"Soldiers' Chorus from Faust"

W22TM

116 HERE WE COME A-WASSAILING
English Folk Song

▶ Experiment with various stickings for the T. Blks. part and write in the sticking that works best for you.

117 THEME FROM "ZAMPA" Page 41
Ferdinand Herold (1791 - 1833)

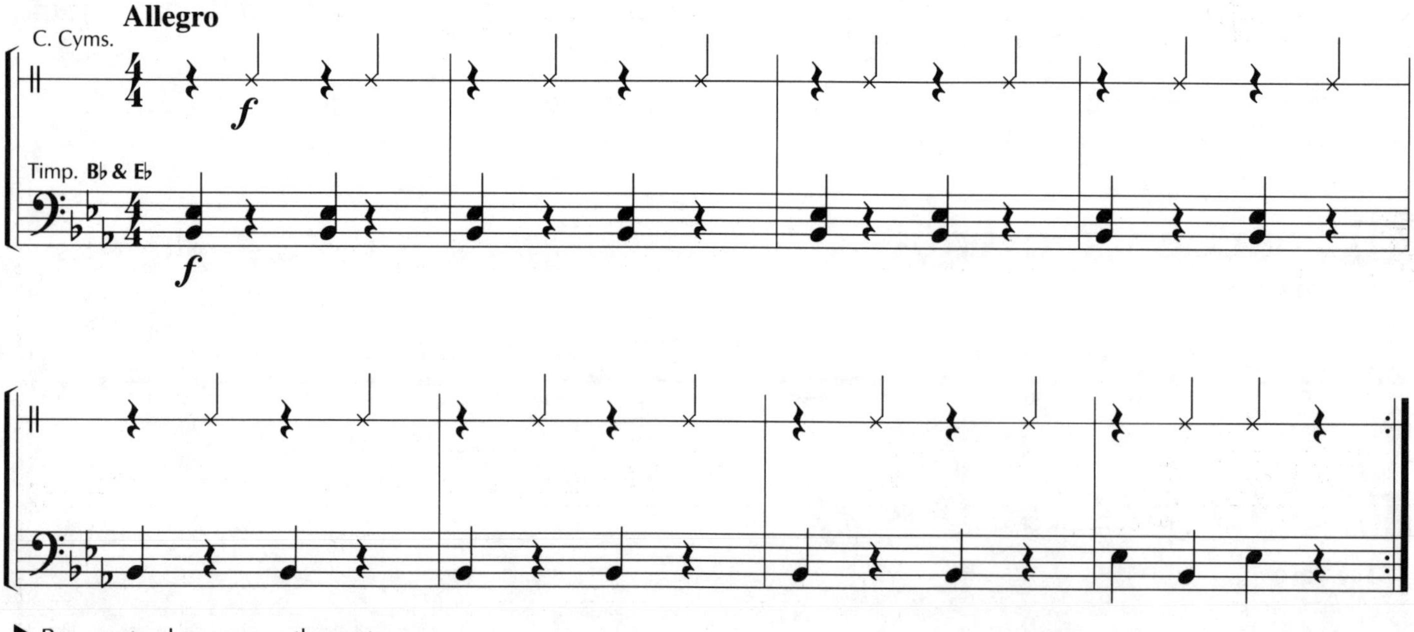

▶ Be sure to dampen on the rests.

W22TM

118 GO FOR EXCELLENCE!

Peter Ilyich Tchaikovsky (1840 - 1893)

Allegretto
"March from the Nutcracker"

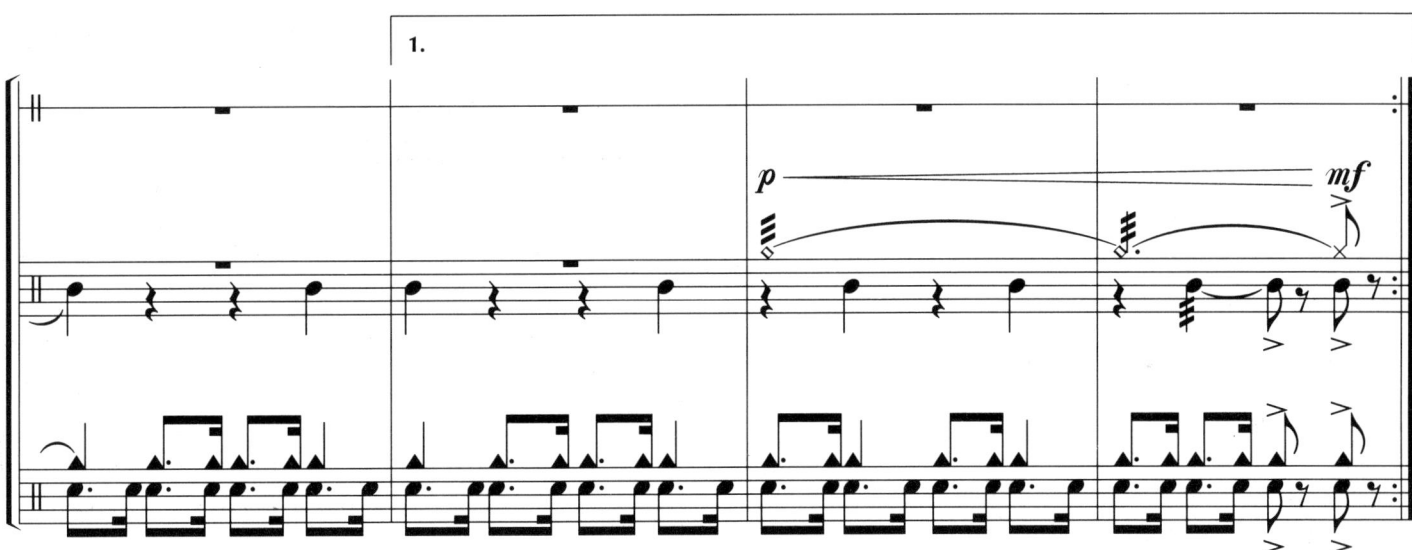

▶ Play the Tri. with two Tri. beaters and the W. Blk. with two rubber mallets. Play the S. Cym. with medium hard yarn mallets.

CABO RICO
Band Arrangement

Maracas
Claves
Suspended Cymbal
Cowbell

Chuck Elledge (b. 1961)

W22TM

RUDIMENTAL REGIMENT
Band Arrangement

Triangle
Wood Block

Bruce Pearson (b. 1942)
and Chuck Elledge (b. 1961)

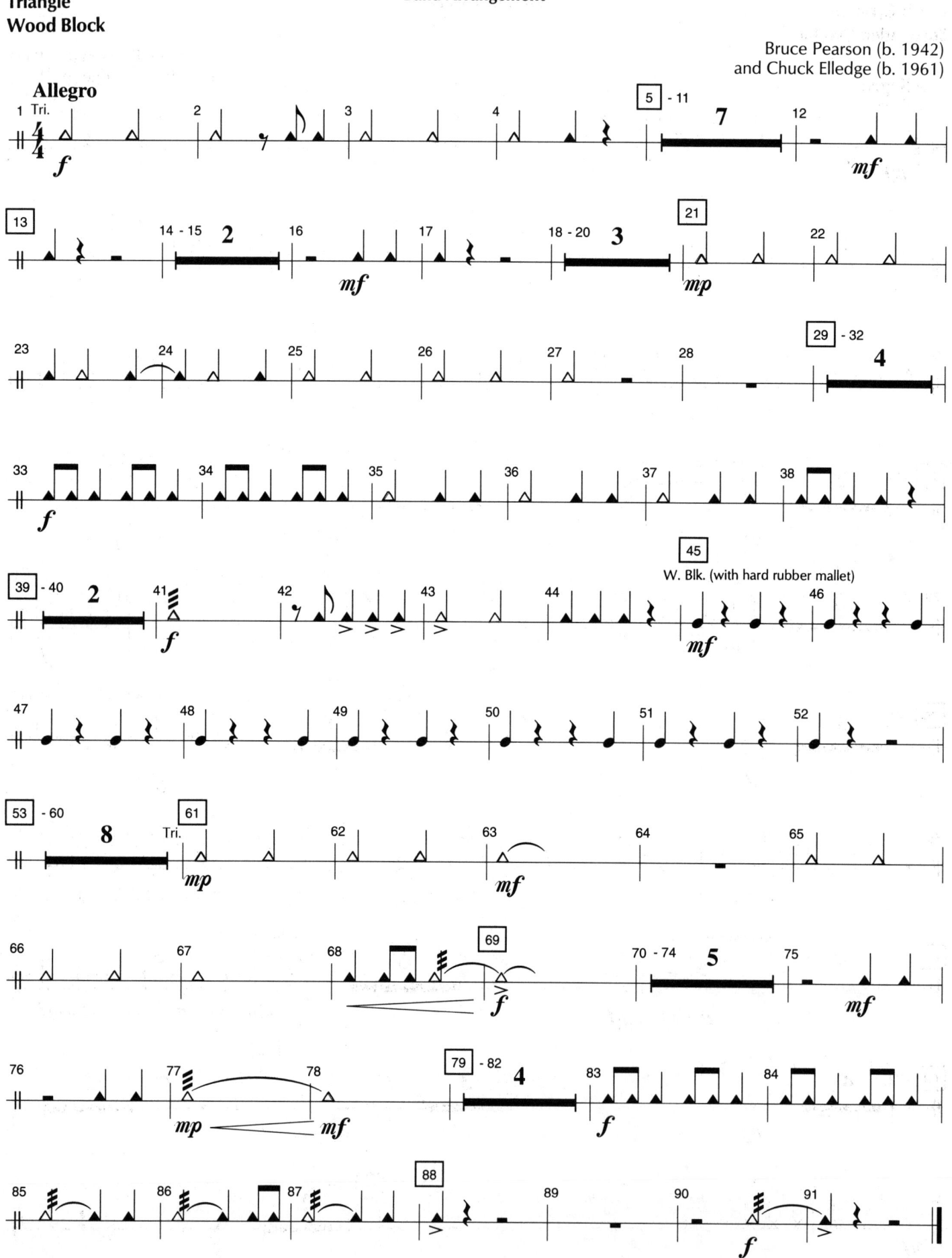

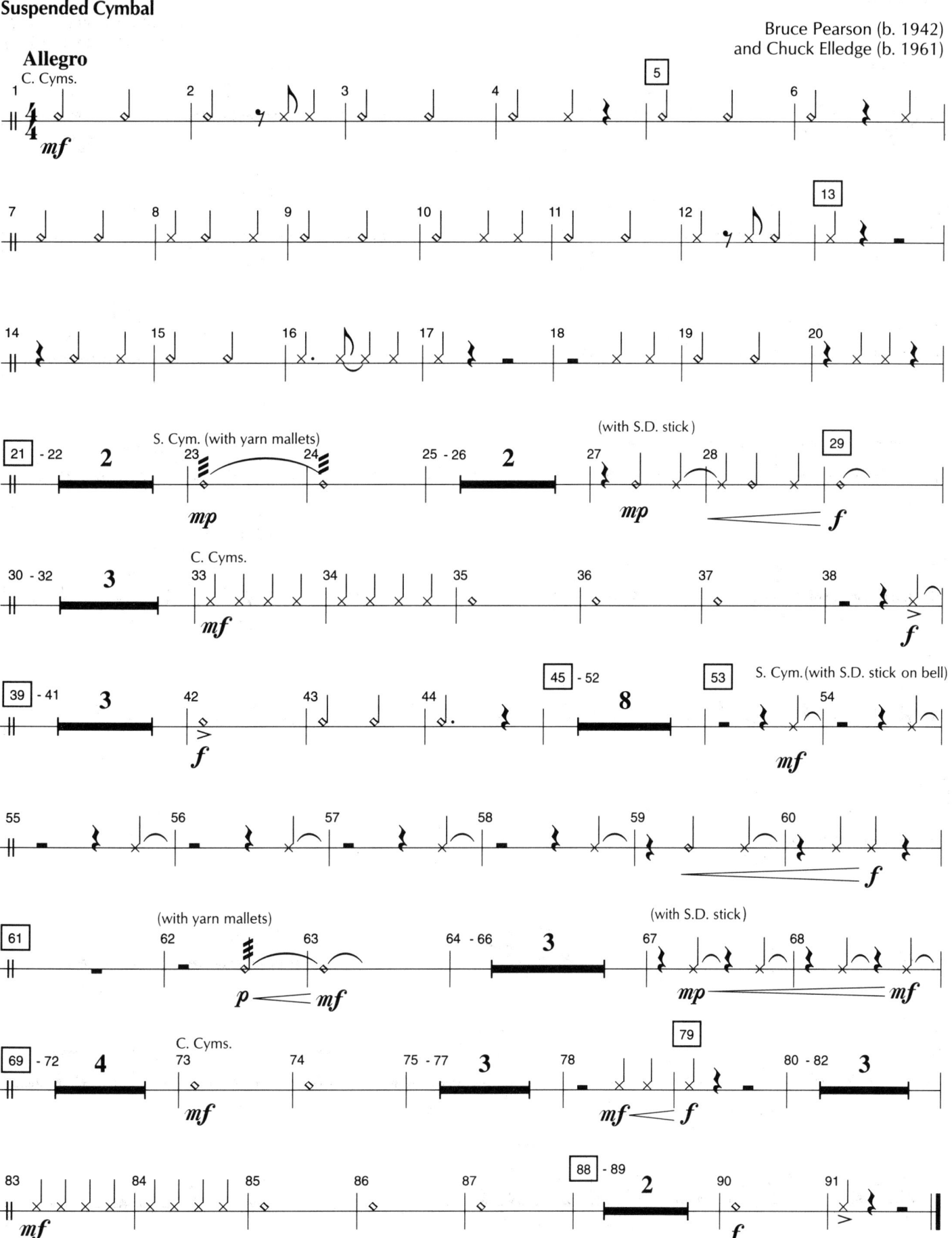

RUDIMENTAL REGIMENT
Band Arrangement

Timpani

Bruce Pearson (b. 1942)
and Chuck Elledge (b. 1961)

FRENCH MARKET BUZZARDS MARCH
Band Arrangement

Triangle
Crash Cymbals

Liberato Gallo
arr. Wendy Barden (b. 1955)

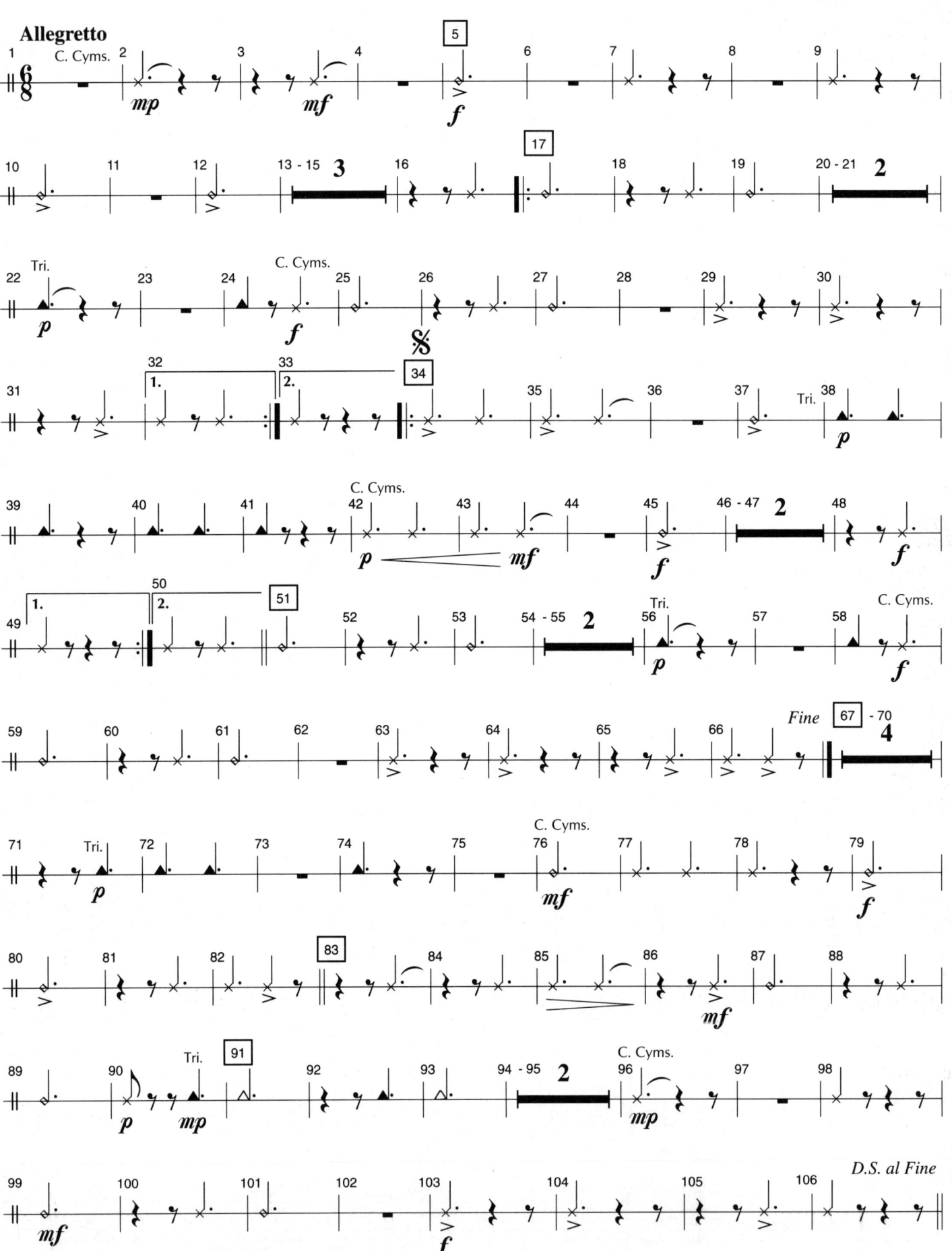

W22TM

FRENCH MARKET BUZZARDS MARCH
Band Arrangement

Timpani

Liberato Gallo
arr. Wendy Barden (b. 1955)

W22TM

JAMAICAN SUNRISE
Percussion Ensemble

Suspended Cymbal
Maracas
Claves
Bongos

Bruce Pearson (b. 1942)

W22TM

▶ To create the stick clicks in measures 24-34, strike the shoulder of one timpani mallet against the shoulder of the other.

EXCELLERATORS - For Percussion Only

INTERVAL — The distance between any two notes.

ARTICULATION — *Staccato* (dot placed above or below note) – Play short and detached.

Playing the Timpani Using a Staccato Stroke

STEP 1
Hold the timpani mallets as you normally would, but tighten the grip at the points where your thumb and index finger grasp the mallet in each hand. Loud and/or fast playing requires you to grip the mallets more tightly to achieve a staccato articulation. Soft and/or slow playing allows a more relaxed staccato grip. You may also tighten your other fingers around the mallets depending on the amount of staccato desired.

STEP 2
Using only your wrist, strike the drum and rebound the mallet off the head immediately. When playing consecutive notes, strike the head at the same spot for each note to achieve a maximum staccato effect.

STEP 3
Use the staccato stroke whenever a clear, cleanly articulated sound is desired, even if staccato marks do not appear in the music. In some cases if time permits, dampening may also be used to achieve a staccato effect.

3 Timp. F & B♭

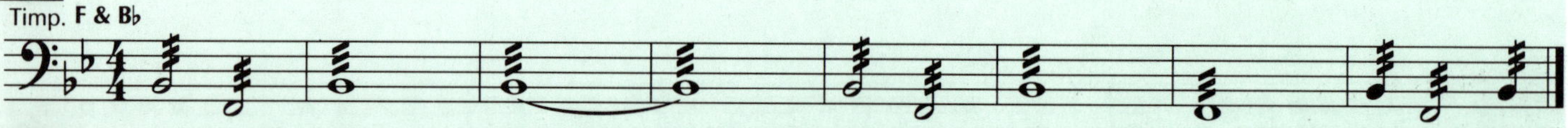

16 Timp. F & C

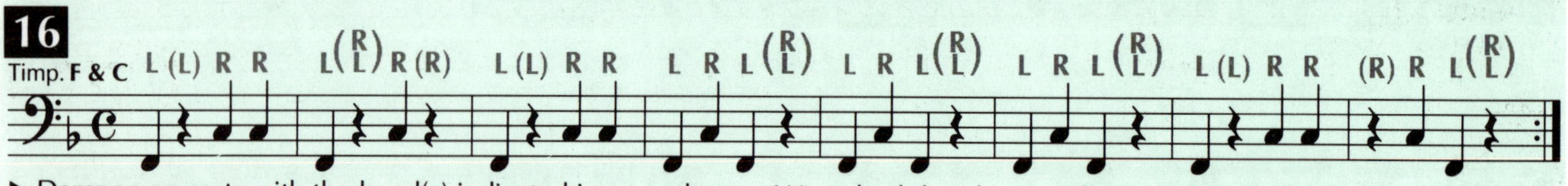

▶ Dampen on rests with the hand(s) indicated in parentheses. When both hands are indicated, dampen both drums (low drum with the left hand and high drum with the right hand).

20A

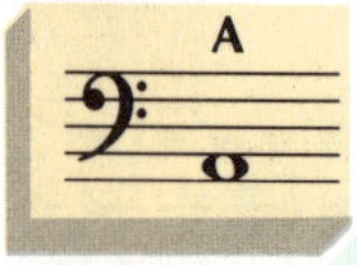

▶ First, play each interval on a mallet percussion instrument, sing it using the numbers, and memorize the sound. Then, play each measure several times. Use only the low drum.

20B

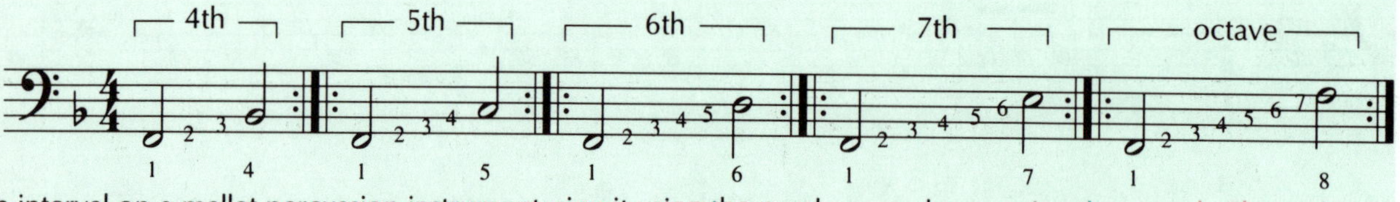

▶ First, play each interval on a mallet percussion instrument, sing it using the numbers, and memorize the sound. Then, play each measure several times. Pedal only the high drum.

28 Timp. F & B♭

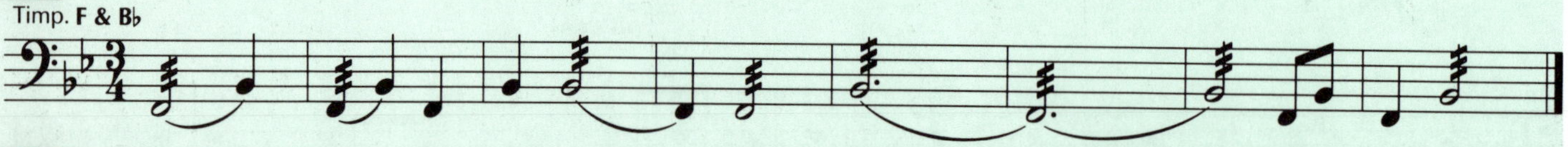

43 Timp. B♭ & E♭

▶ Use staccato strokes. Dampen on the rests.

Rhythm Studies

Rhythm Studies

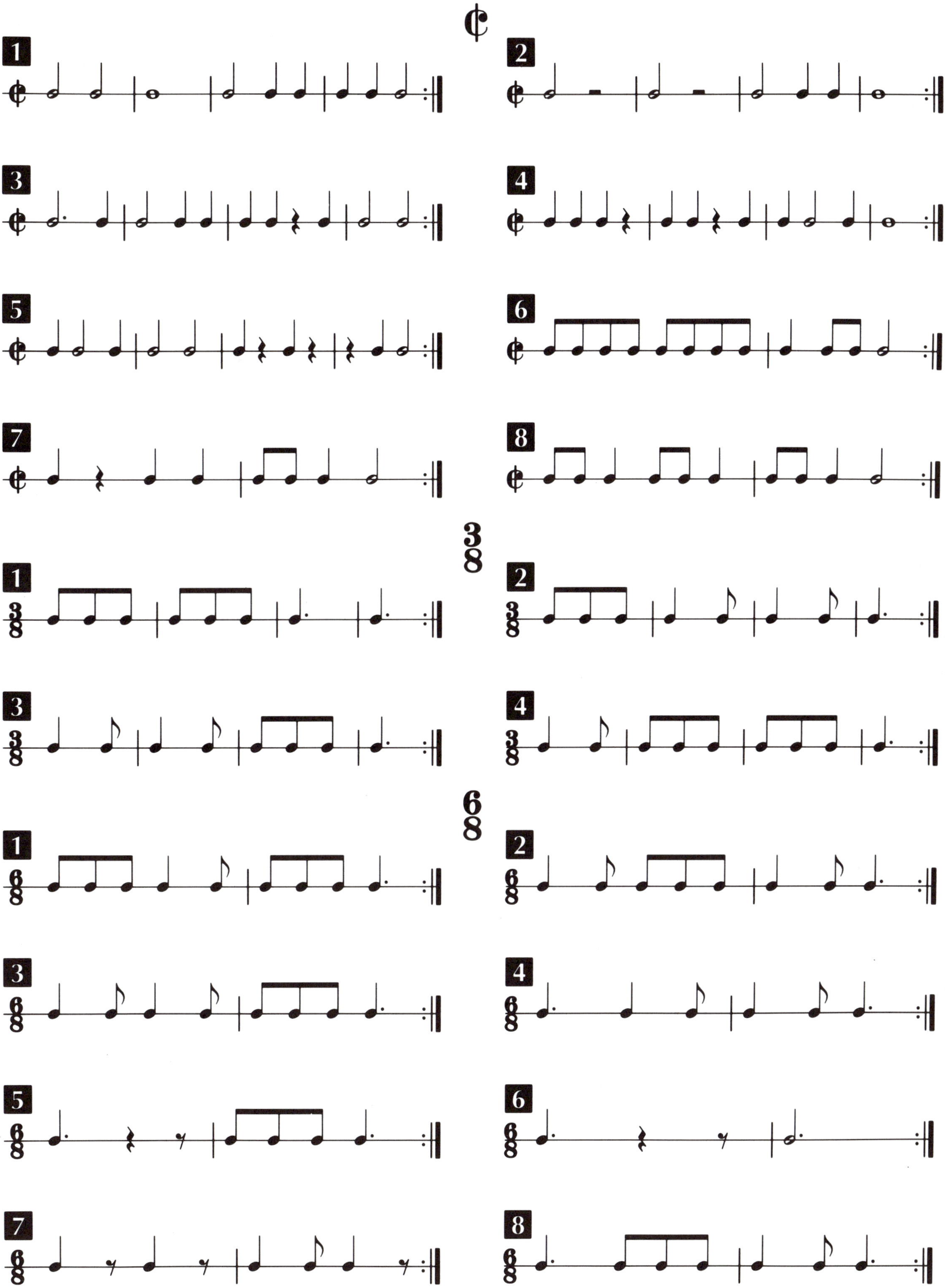

STANDARD OF EXCELLENCE

EXERCISE 2
- ☐ pitch/rhythm
- ☐ pulse
- ☐ sticking
- ☐ Timp. tech.

EXERCISE 5
- ☐ rhythm
- ☐ dynamics
- ☐ *D.C. al Fine*
- ☐ Tri. tech.

EXERCISE 6
- ☐ pitch/rhythm
- ☐ grip/posture
- ☐ stroke
- ☐ roll

EXERCISE 7
- ☐ pitch/rhythm
- ☐ *ritardando*
- ☐ dynamics
- ☐ 1st/2nd endings

EXERCISE 12
- ☐ pitch/rhythm
- ☐ pulse
- ☐ sticking
- ☐ Timp. tech.

EXERCISE 16
- ☐ pitch/rhythm
- ☐ sticking
- ☐ dampening
- ☐ grip/posture

EXERCISE 21
- ☐ pitch/rhythm
- ☐ dynamics
- ☐ tempo
- ☐ Timp. tech.

EXERCISE 24
- ☐ pitch/rhythm
- ☐ pulse
- ☐ ⌒
- ☐ Timp. tech.

EXERCISE 28
- ☐ pitch/rhythm
- ☐ sticking
- ☐ rolls
- ☐ slurs

EXERCISE 29
- ☐ pitch/rhythm
- ☐ pulse
- ☐ *D.C. al Fine*
- ☐ Timp. tech.

EXERCISE 33
- ☐ pitch/rhythm
- ☐ grip/posture
- ☐ rolls
- ☐ dampening

EXERCISE 35
- ☐ pitch/rhythm
- ☐ dynamics
- ☐ rolls
- ☐ Timp. tech.

EXERCISE 36
- ☐ pitch/rhythm
- ☐ sticking
- ☐ dampening
- ☐ rolls

EXERCISE 39
- ☐ pitch/rhythm
- ☐ dynamics
- ☐ *accelerando*
- ☐ Timp. tech.

EXERCISE 42
- ☐ rhythm
- ☐ time signatures
- ☐ ⌒
- ☐ S. Cym. tech.

EXERCISE 45
- ☐ pitch/rhythm
- ☐ rolls
- ☐ slurs
- ☐ dampening

EXERCISE 47
- ☐ rhythm
- ☐ grip/posture
- ☐ rolls
- ☐ slur

EXERCISE 51
- ☐ rhythm
- ☐ repeats
- ☐ tempo
- ☐ Tri. tech.

EXERCISE 53
- ☐ rhythm
- ☐ tempo
- ☐ rolls
- ☐ Tamb. tech.

EXERCISE 57
- ☐ pitch/rhythm
- ☐ stroke
- ☐ sticking
- ☐ dampening

EXERCISE 62
- ☐ rhythm
- ☐ dynamics
- ☐ tempo
- ☐ C. Cyms. tech.

EXERCISE 65
- ☐ rhythm
- ☐ *D.C. al Fine*
- ☐ Tri. tech.
- ☐ Tamb. tech.

EXERCISE 67
- ☐ pitch/rhythm
- ☐ rolls
- ☐ slurs
- ☐ repeat

EXERCISE 69
- ☐ rhythm
- ☐ pulse
- ☐ repeats
- ☐ Bongo tech.

EXERCISE 72
- ☐ rhythm
- ☐ pulse
- ☐ accents
- ☐ Bongo tech.

EXERCISE 76
- ☐ pitch/rhythm
- ☐ rolls
- ☐ Tamb. tech.
- ☐ Timp. tech.

EXERCISE 77
- ☐ rhythm
- ☐ Marc. tech.
- ☐ Claves tech.
- ☐ Timp. tech.

EXERCISE 81
- ☐ pitch/rhythm
- ☐ dynamics
- ☐ *ritardando*
- ☐ Timp. tech.

EXERCISE 87
- ☐ pitch/rhythm
- ☐ long rest
- ☐ C. Cyms. tech.
- ☐ Timp. tech.

EXERCISE 88
- ☐ pitch/rhythm
- ☐ time signatures
- ☐ W. Blk. tech.
- ☐ Tri. tech.

EXERCISE 91
- ☐ rhythm
- ☐ pulse
- ☐ coordination
- ☐ *D.C. al Coda*

EXERCISE 92
- ☐ pitch/rhythm
- ☐ pulse
- ☐ sticking
- ☐ Timp. tech.

EXERCISE 96
- ☐ rhythm
- ☐ dynamics
- ☐ accents
- ☐ Tamb. tech.

EXERCISE 100
- ☐ rhythm
- ☐ dynamics
- ☐ repeats
- ☐ W. Blk. tech.

EXERCISE 101
- ☐ rhythm
- ☐ pulse
- ☐ dynamics
- ☐ Tamb. tech.

EXERCISE 106
- ☐ pitch/rhythm
- ☐ pulse
- ☐ accents
- ☐ rolls

EXERCISE 111
- ☐ rhythm
- ☐ dynamics
- ☐ accents
- ☐ C. B. tech.

EXERCISE 115
- ☐ rhythm
- ☐ pulse
- ☐ repeats
- ☐ C. Cyms. tech.

EXERCISE 116
- ☐ rhythm
- ☐ pulse
- ☐ S. B. tech.
- ☐ T. Blks. tech.

EXERCISE 118
- ☐ rhythm
- ☐ Tamb. tech.
- ☐ Tri. tech.
- ☐ W. Blk. tech.